T0149475

REAL LOVE IS
"for Real"

A guide for teens, young adults, and others in search
of authentic love: reflections, stories, examples, and
a plan to help you find Real Love.

PAM HEIL

BALBOA
PRESS

A DIVISION OF HAY HOUSE

Copyright © 2017 Pam Heil.

All rights reserved. No part of this book may be used or reproduced by any means, graphic, electronic, or mechanical, including photocopying, recording, taping or by any information storage retrieval system without the written permission of the author except in the case of brief quotations embodied in critical articles and reviews.

Scripture texts in this work are taken from the New American Bible, revised edition© 2010, 1991, 1986, 1970 Confraternity of Christian Doctrine, Washington, D.C. and are used by permission of the copyright owner. All Rights Reserved. No part of the New American Bible may be reproduced in any form without permission in writing from the copyright owner.

Balboa Press books may be ordered through booksellers or by contacting:

Balboa Press
A Division of Hay House
1663 Liberty Drive
Bloomington, IN 47403
www.balboapress.com
1 (877) 407-4847

Because of the dynamic nature of the Internet, any web addresses or links contained in this book may have changed since publication and may no longer be valid. The views expressed in this work are solely those of the author and do not necessarily reflect the views of the publisher, and the publisher hereby disclaims any responsibility for them.

The author of this book does not dispense medical advice or prescribe the use of any technique as a form of treatment for physical, emotional, or medical problems without the advice of a physician, either directly or indirectly. The intent of the author is only to offer information of a general nature to help you in your quest for emotional and spiritual well-being. In the event you use any of the information in this book for yourself, which is your constitutional right, the author and the publisher assume no responsibility for your actions.

Any people depicted in stock imagery provided by Thinkstock are models, and such images are being used for illustrative purposes only.
Certain stock imagery © Thinkstock.

Print information available on the last page.

ISBN: 978-1-5043-9076-7 (sc)
ISBN: 978-1-5043-9077-4 (hc)
ISBN: 978-1-5043-9075-0 (e)

Library of Congress Control Number: 2017916787

Balboa Press rev. date: 10/27/2017

A wonderful extension of her message from her speaking engagements which empower teens to choose chastity: formulating a morality based on love, not sex.

Contents

Section III. The Plan

Foreword

The world in which you live is vastly different than any other. There is very little considered sacred. Advertising and social media have left no subject taboo. What does it means to be a man? What does it means to be a woman? How to dress? How to talk? How to date? These used to be questions with clear-cut answers. Behaviors used to have boundaries: everybody knew where and when certain things were appropriate, and when they were not. Some things were actually considered wrong.

Today, there is so much confusion: about how to establish relationships with the opposite sex, about being gay or straight, about if we should have sex on the first date or wait a few weeks, or even what constitute sex. Locker room talk, profanity and vulgarity, previously acceptable only in single gender situations, have gone public. Pornography is now a multibillion-dollar business generating more income than all professional sports. Commercials about condoms, feminine hygiene products, and erectile dysfunction are so commonplace that most of you don't even know that those things used to "not ever be talked about in public," or at least in mixed company.

Regardless, of how we got to where we are, downward trends in our society might suggest that we should consider some changes. Teen pregnancy, depression, teen suicide, sexual transmitted diseases, AIDS, divorce, domestic violence, sex abuse, date rape, and varied addictions are just a few of the real problems which are bringing so much pain to our world.

Today, we live in a world in which most of us are so busy, we feel disconnected and frazzled. Most feel lonely and unloved more than we feel safe and secure. The numbers of us who are taking pills to alleviate our pain or mask our unhappiness are making pharmaceutical companies wealthy. We are trying to fill our voids with all kinds of things, which begin to control us, like food, alcohol, gambling, sex, and other addictions.

What we all need is to feel loved. We need to love ourselves enough to restore a respect for ourselves and for one another. We need to recognize that none of us is perfect, but that we all possess different gifts and talents. Because of that reality, I believe we're going to find happiness as a human race, only when we discover ways to fill each others voids and to share each others strengths: my strengths should fill someone else's weaknesses and their strengths should compensate for my weaknesses. In order for that to happen, we need to find each other, to meet each other, to know each other, so we can complete one another. We can only discover the beauty of being interdependent by being in relationship with others. We need one another to grow physically, emotionally, and spiritually.

When we become less threatened by others, when we become less competitive, when we learn to build each other up rather than to tear each other down, we will have learned how to support each other on this difficult journey of life, and life will become easier for us all. If we are going to peacefully coexist, we must learn to love one another.

What the world needs most is real, healthy, love! This book is a conversation, which I hope, will help you to accept the call to do your part to save our world by being better at loving.

Introduction

People asked why I would want to write a book about love. Aren't there enough of those around? Probably! However, this book is geared to helping you find authentic love, real love, in a world deprived, in so many ways, of our fundamental need as humans: to love and to be loved.

This book about love is written because I am concerned about the vast number of us who struggle with the belief that we are unlovable, unworthy of being loved, or incapable of loving. People need help to heal and to connect with those in their families, schools, places of employment, neighborhoods, and churches. Relationships are broken, and people do not know how to fix them. If we don't believe love is possible, then we can't create it, or spread it, or share it.

I am genuinely concerned about the "disconnect" in our world. Even though people are "plugged in" by the media, the most dominant emotion for both young and old seems to be loneliness. How can we overcome this emotion that leads people to various ways of negative coping skills? So many of us have turned to food, material possessions, alcohol and other drugs, both prescribed and illegal, to deal with our pain. The source of that pain for many is the desire to be seen, valued, and respected: so many people feel invisible and unloved, even insignificant.

I believe each person was created good and gifted. If all of us believed that about ourselves, perhaps, we would take the first step to sharing that goodness and giftedness with our world. If we don't do our part to create the beautiful mosaic that would exist if we each recognized our gifts and shared them with our world, there will be a gaping hole in our universe, which could be filled with anger, frustration, aggression, and downright meanness, instead of peace and love.

In scripture, St. Paul calls us one body. If that were true, when one of us hurts, we all would hurt. When one of us rejoices, we would all feel joy. For this intimacy to be possible, we must be in relationship with one another: eyeball-to-eyeball, heart to heart.

The activity of putting a puzzle together with family or friends is kind of a dying pastime. People used to sit around talking and working to put together a thousand piece puzzle of a beautiful piece of art, over hours, days or even weeks. During that time, many topics of conversation would surface as everyone worked together to look for the pieces, which were designed to perfectly fit together. Often times, everyone would be frantically trying to find a certain piece and would swear it had been lost…dropped on the floor, eaten by the dog, whatever! The piece would usually show up, but sometimes, despite all the effort, that huge puzzle would be missing just one piece. One piece, which had been misplaced, displaced, overlooked, or lost was gone. All eyes would be saddened, and people would be frustrated by the gaping hole, caused by the one missing piece, and ruining the beautiful masterpiece.

I don't want that missing piece to be you.

I want you to find the love, to trust the love, and to share the love that is you with our world.

Pam Heil

Empowered to Love Ministries

National Speaker with the National Federation of Youth Ministers

Speaker with Youth to Youth International

Certified Christian Counselor

Nationally Certified Youth Minister and Campus Minister

Young Adult Minister

Family First Coordinator

Teacher and Coach

Section I. The Ideal

Believe in Real Love

1 Cor. 13:4-8

Love is patient, love is kind. It is not jealous, [love] is not pompous, it is not inflated, [5] it is not rude, it does not seek its own interests, it is not quick-tempered, it does not brood over injury, [6] it does not rejoice over wrongdoing but rejoices with the truth. [7] It bears all things, believes all things, hopes all things, endures all things.

Love never fails.

New American Bible Revised Edition (NABRE)

Chapter 1. Is Real Love Possible in Today's World?

People have been heartbroken so many times by broken relationships that many doubt that authentic love is even possible. If we doubt something is possible, we cannot make it happen. When we believe in something, we can strive for it. We can start over after we have been hurt by betrayal, abuse, abandonment, or infidelity, but first we must believe that real love is "for real," that it is possible to find in today's world.

I believe real love exists in our world. I have seen it. I have experienced it. I have been inspired by it. I have felt it. Below are some examples of what I have witnessed in my own life.

My "kids" all seem to truly care for each other. Kevin, the oldest has always connected in a special way with the needs of his younger siblings and cousins. Even when he speaks to them, he bends down to their level, making each one feel his genuine concern for them. He seemed to naturally assume the role of caregiver. Maybe his kindness was "caught" by the others, because they are all very good at sharing and looking out for one another with genuine love. The hugs between Elly and Hannah, and Lukas and Levi, are an expression of a beautiful sisterly and brotherly love. When Kathleen runs into my arms, I feel the love. Even when Brandon runs away from my hugs, I feel the love in the game of chasing him until I catch him to sneak a squeeze or a pat on the head.

My Allison is a fiercely competitive athlete who strives for excellence in all that she does. She absolutely hates to lose, and in the category of love, she always seems to win.

When she was six, I observed her noticing her little sister shivering in her lightweight sweater, and without any hesitation, she removed her warm sweatshirt and gave it to Kathleen. That same little girl insisted that I open her Christmas present for me before she opened any of hers; she was so excited to give me the Browns gloves she had purchased, because she knew I was a crazy fan!

One night we took the "kids" to a baseball game. Each child received a free baseball as a promotion that night. When we were driving home, one of the girls realized she didn't have her ball and began to cry. It apparently had fallen out of her bag. We looked and looked for it, but concluded that she had probably lost it at the game.

Allison knew how sad Elly was and when someone around her is sad, she always seems to personally feel their heartache. After arriving home and having snacks, I noticed Allison was not with the others. I found her in my van in the garage crawling around looking for the missing ball. Even though others had seemed to move on, she was still trying to heal someone else's pain.

True love is other-centered. It is selfless. Allison possesses a true servant heart. She knows how to love.

♥▲♥▲♥▲♥▲ ♥ ▲♥▲♥▲♥▲♥

One of the Core Team members of my Youth Group, who has been confined to a wheelchair for years, was a part of his high school football team as the team manager for four years. John had attended all practices and served his teammates in the many, sometimes gross ways a manager does.

On senior night, his team wanted to show how invaluable John was to them. The quarterback called John's number when they got into the Red Zone. John rolled out onto the field and took the handoff from his quarterback. Both sides of the entire stadium erupted into deafening cheers when John drove his wheelchair, into the end zone and scored. The love and appreciation of a team, the support of the fans, the thoughtfulness of a crowd of strangers were beautiful to behold.

Love is empathetic; we try to put ourselves into the shoes of another. Love is kind.

♥▲▼▲▼▲▼▲♥▲▼▲▼▲▼▲♥

I attended a memorial dinner for Peter, one of our young diocesan leaders who had been a dog handler in the Marines. Dog handlers are teamed with another Marine, which happens to be a dog, and together they go out on the roads and into buildings to find explosives before they explode and kill others.

Duke had sniffed out a roadside bomb, and he and Peter were doing their job of waiting for the Marines, who were trained to defuse bombs, to arrive. While he was waiting, Peter took out his Bible as he often did. It calmed him to pray.

An assassin shot and killed Peter while he was praying his Bible, sitting with his dog, Duke.

The loss we all felt was horrific. Peter was a selfless, gentle soul who loved his God, his family and friends, and his fellow Marines. He loved life, and offered true friendship and loyalty to others. He brought joy into the room because he appreciated others and celebrated life: one of his favorite mottos was, "Life is short, eat dessert first."

The surviving officer, the dog was the guest of honor at the memorial ceremony. The dog suffered severely from the trauma of having lost his buddy, the young man who had trained him, served by his side, and loved him. During the dinner, the dog was presented as a gift to Peter's family who had chosen to adopt him.

Although the grief stricken Duke had been traumatized and quite aloof toward humans since his beloved Marine had died, something special happened that night. Duke immediately went to Peter's little brother and nuzzled close to him; he looked so much like his big brother, the Marine, who had died by Duke's side on the battlefield.

Duke instinctively sensed the love of family, that connectedness which cannot be broken by death, and he immediately became part of Peter's family. He followed them everywhere; he felt safe, loved, and connected as he had felt with Peter, his trainer, his buddy, and his friend.

Oh, by the way, after Peter's funeral there was a city-wide reception in a very large gathering hall. The packed house of people, who came to honor and thank this young Marine, were treated to tables and tables and tables of homemade desserts, donated by the community. Hanging from the wall was a huge banner saying: "Life is short; eat dessert first." We can all learn so much from one another!

Real love appreciates and celebrates the goodness in life. It recognizes that we are all one family.

Family, ideally, is the first experience of God's love: a place where we feel safe, appreciated, loved, and connected.

♥▲♥▲♥▲♥▲♥▲♥▲♥▲♥▲♥

I met a lady in the hospital who had not left the building since her husband had been hospitalized ten days before. Even though the doctor had told her that her life-long love could be in a coma for a very long time, she patiently waited. (She calmly and lovingly told me, "I want to be here when he wakes up.")

With true love, one's joy comes from being truly present to one another.

♥▲♥▲♥▲♥▲♥▲♥▲♥▲♥▲♥

I attended the funeral of a man whose wife of 64 years shared these words with me, through tear-filled eyes, "I already miss him so, so much." (Not only were they married that long, but they worked together every day in their real estate business and "never got tired of each other.") She chuckled as she told me about his sometimes-irritating behaviors. She sadly shared their struggles over the deaths of a couple of their children, and acknowledged that they had worked at their marriage everyday, because neither of them was without flaws.

Because nobody is perfect, focusing on the good in another is the way to love perfectly.

♥▲♥▲♥▲♥▲♥♥▲♥▲♥▲♥▲♥

I admired my 96 year old Uncle who rode the bus to visit his wife everyday at the Alzheimer's clinic to share three meals a day with her. She didn't recognize him, but when his sons tried to get him to take better care of himself and to visit her less frequently, he sternly stated, "She may not know me, but I know her."

Real love does not expect to be rewarded; the reward is actually in the love. Uncle Tony saw Aunt Louise through the eyes of unending, unconditional love.

♥▲♥▲♥▲♥▲♥♥▲♥▲♥▲♥▲♥

My husband and I were blessed with four children, and we would do anything for them. We made them work. They had chores. We had rules, and we held our children accountable.

We accepted their anger when they didn't get their way. We forgave them when they hurt us with their words. We celebrated their accomplishments, and we encouraged them when they failed. We held them when they cried, and we tried to challenge them, without judging them.

We understood they were imperfect like we are, but beautifully and wonderfully made like each of us is.

We set boundaries and were consistent in certain expectations of behavior, which we believed would guide them to become the people they were created to be. We sometimes said, "NO."

Sometimes, God says, "No" to our prayers, and when he does,

"NO" becomes a love word. Real love recognizes that sometimes compromise is necessary for the good of others.

❤️▲❤️▲❤️▲❤️▲❤️▲❤️▲❤️▲❤️▲❤️

Sixteen of my cousins travelled from Ohio to North Carolina to attend my cousin's funeral. Despite the threat of winter storms, we each felt we just had to be there to celebrate Ray's life. Our extended family had celebrated a family reunion for 71 years, starting when my father and all his brothers and brothers-in law returned safely from war. Because of these annual week long gatherings we became more than cousins; we were friends.

His adult sons had not fully understood the love of my father's and their grandfather's family, until they felt our love and support in their grief. Through our presence, our hugs, and our memories and stories about their Dad, they felt the real love we as family felt for our cousin. The younger son cried when we left and said, "Now I understand why Dad would never miss the family reunion in Ohio."

When real love is present, there is compassion, shared emotions, shared experience, and the gift of time spent together.

❤️▲❤️▲❤️▲❤️▲❤️▲❤️▲❤️▲❤️▲❤️

We sponsored an annual Valentine's Dance event at my Church for older generations and our high school students. The couples shared with our teens the wisdom about why their marriages had lasted for so many decades. The husband of one of the couples who had been married over 50 years had recently died, and the wife explained to us that the things she missed the most about her husband were the very things that used to drive her crazy when they were first married. When past irritants can bring you a memory, which makes you smile, we can realize that love is a decision.

When we read about men and women in the military who go into war to attempt to bring peace and justice to persecuted or oppressed people, when we see first responders, police officers, firefighters, ministers, medical personnel, and missionaries run toward danger to rescue others and to treat their wounds, while we run away and try to escape danger and pain, we can begin to get a picture of what real love is.

There was a quote in the movie, Pearl Harbor, which stated, "There is nothing more powerful than the heart of a volunteer." Historically, and recently, we have witnessed volunteers leaving their homes to rescue people from hurricanes, floods, fires, earthquakes, or terrorist attacks, proving that real love exists.

Humankind is caring for one another; people are valuing each other despite differences; people are coming to the aid of strangers. Despite media reports, we must believe in the general goodness of most people.

We must believe something is possible before we can make it happen. If you ask any professional athlete, any successful actor or actress, performer or entertainer, they will tell you that they dreamt it, believed it to be possible, and worked hard to attain their goals and fulfill their dreams.

Real love does exist. You can be a part of it, you can experience it, you can make it a reality in your life, but first you must recognize it for what it is: the ideal and a real possibility.

What do all of my examples of authentic love have in common? Each of these depicted unselfish acts of kindness. Each involved sacrifices willingly given, without any desire for attention, recognition, or reward. Each involved a decision, rooted in the oneness of authentic love relationships. Each conveyed a desire to be close to a loved one, to be what they needed us to be in a given moment. Each recognized that we are intimately connected by our shared humanity, and we need to share our goodness with each other to make our world a more loving place.

Above are some of my examples of real love. If you look around,

I hope you will see examples in your life, too. I believe real love is possible because no matter what changes have happened in the world, we were still created to love and to be loved.

Real love grows from truly intimate connectedness: when two people are so close that when one of them feels joy, the other celebrates, and when one of them cries, the other one tastes the salt of their tears.

Questions to ponder:

1. Where have you witnessed authentic love? Please don't say," Never." Think about it.

2. What is one thing you can do to help someone who you know is feeling down, isolated, or unimportant feel loved?

Love is what we need to grow, to flourish, to thrive.

Chapter 2. Love Is What We Need

We all need to be loved, to be able to receive and give love freely, to find the joy we were created to experience in our shared humanity. Failure to thrive is an actual medical condition which comes from touch deprivation, often felt by elderly who live alone, infirm people who are confined to their homes because of a lack of mobility, or infants in third world countries who live in orphanages.

Physical illness and weakness result from a disconnection that was never meant to be. Depression and anxiety are rampant in parts of our population, which are so isolated that people have nobody with whom to share the ups and downs of life.

Life can be like a roller coaster: up and down, up and down, up and down. Have you noticed that the ups are more fun when they are shared with others, and the downs are easier to handle when we have someone to lean on or to help us carry our burdens.

Imagine how empty you would feel if you hit the winning shot in a championship game, and you were awarded the trophy in a gym all by yourself: no teammates to jump on you, no fans to cheer and go crazy, no parents to brag, "That's my kid!"

Imagine, you were asked to prom by the love of your life, or you were accepted into your dream college, or you scored your ideal score on the ACT or SAT, or you did your personal best in your sport, and you went to call your best friend or your parents to share the good news, and nobody picked up.

Happiness, accomplishments, and milestones attained are just more joyful when shared with others. That is because we humans were created to be in relationship with one another.

Now imagine getting cut from a team, or not making the lead

in a play for which you worked so hard, or having an accident and being stranded on the side of the road and nobody "picking up". What if you had to experience a death, or a divorce, or a breakup, without a friend to talk with, cry with, or pray with?

Get my drift? Life is not meant to live alone. John Donne wrote, "No man is an island." Isolation is not good! Why do you think one of the most horrible punishments in prison, or in prisoner of war camps is solitary confinement?

Think back when you were a kid and you were put in "time out"…didn't five minutes seem like a very long time? Didn't you wonder if anybody loved you?

Maybe you have read an obituary in which it states, "Mr. or Mrs. so and so died surrounded by family and friends whom they loved."

Maybe, you have written in a card or prayed for a loved one, "May you be comforted by the memories of the one you love."

Maybe, you have lost a friend in an automobile accident or from a drug overdose and the grief seems as though it will never end…but love can comfort, and love can heal, and the three F's, faith, family, and friends will help you survive.

Love is what we need, and its power is amazing!

Questions to ponder:

1. When were you comforted or inspired by the words or actions of another?

2. Was there something in your past that you didn't think was survivable that taught you something about the power of love?

Pam Heil

"If" by Rudyard Kipling

If you can keep your head when all about you
Are losing theirs and blaming it on you,
If you can trust yourself when all men doubt you,
But make allowance for their doubting too;
If you can wait and not be tired by waiting,
Or being lied about, don't deal in lies,
Or being hated, don't give way to hating,
And yet don't look too good, nor talk too wise:
If you can dream—and not make dreams your master;
If you can think—and not make thoughts your aim;
If you can meet with Triumph and Disaster
And treat those two impostors just the same;
If you can bear to hear the truth you've spoken
Twisted by knaves to make a trap for fools,
Or watch the things you gave your life to, broken,
And stoop and build 'em up with worn-out tools:
If you can make one heap of all your winnings
And risk it on one turn of pitch-and-toss,
And lose, and start again at your beginnings
And never breathe a word about your loss;
If you can force your heart and nerve and sinew
To serve your turn long after they are gone,
And so hold on when there is nothing in you
Except the Will which says to them: 'Hold on!'
If you can talk with crowds and keep your virtue,
Or walk with Kings—nor lose the common touch,
If neither foes nor loving friends can hurt you,
If all men count with you, but none too much;
If you can fill the unforgiving minute
With sixty seconds' worth of distance run,
Yours is the Earth and everything that's in it,
And—which is more—you'll be a Man, my son!

Chapter 3. I Tried It, and It Hurt!

Love is awesome! It is wonderful! But because we are human, with love comes risk and often pain. Is it worth it to try to love, to open yourself up to another, to become one spirit with another? I believe it is.

When I was a junior in high school, I was in love. He made me feel beautiful and special. We were going to marry after college. We went to different schools our junior years of college, but he was in school with my best friend at the time. She was engaged to her fiancé who was at war. The four of us double dated a lot before he was deployed. I trusted them with all of my heart. Because we were gone, they often hung out together, but I was cool with that. She loved her fiancé, and mine loved me, after all.

They became each other's best friends and one thing led to another and at Christmas, when the four of us were together, there was a weird feeling present. We discovered that my best friend and my fiancé had cheated on us together.

I wanted to die. When I went back to college, the pain didn't go away. I planned my suicide and went out to get drunk for the first time, to give myself the courage to do it.

I was picked up at a bar; I was very wasted. The guy took me to his place, and I figured I knew what was coming, (Guys told me that drunk girls can be easy), and I was OK with that, because I was going to die that night anyway.

The guy who picked me up turned out to be a priest who routinely went to campus bars to help people he thought were in trouble. He helped me get sober, held me while I cried, prayed with me, and convinced me that life was still worth living. Over the next several months he helped me heal.

Yes, love can hurt, but is it worth the risk? YES! I think of how many years of love with my husband and family I would have missed, had God not dropped Father Fred into my life that night.

Questions to ponder:

1. Have you ever trained for a sport, or practiced something so many hours that you thought you were going to drop, but still pushed on, and either attained a personal best or won a competition?

2. Have you ever heard, "If at first you don't succeed, try, try again," a common lesson learned as a child. I say, "Try, try again to love, even if you have been deeply hurt or wounded in your quest for happiness."

Proverbs: 10:12

Hatred stirs up conflict, but love covers all wrongs.

(NABRE)

Chapter 4. Looking at Love a Different Way

Love isn't just a onetime deal or a onetime chance. I want to show you how love can evolve, how even love which seems to be gone can be restored, how God sharing his mercy with us can help us view love in a different way.

My family had some issues. I guess all families do. However, my mom had some deep love issues and some deep trust issues. She was unable to overcome some insecurities rooted in her family upbringing, and she projected many of her negative emotions onto me.

I did not feel loved by her. That is a horrible feeling for a daughter to feel toward her mother. As it turned out, it was not an imagined feeling.

When I graduated from college, Dad asked me to come home because my Mom was dying. When I went to her bedside, I asked her why she hated me, and she honestly said, "Because your Dad loves you more than he loves me." She was jealous and insecure: Dad and I loved sports, understood each other, shared so many interests, and Mom put limits on his love. She didn't realize that there is always enough love to go around when the love is real.

Mom did not die at that time, and as a result of the painful, revealing conversation of that night, there came years of awkwardness between Mom and me. Two years ago, Mom did die, and during the last month of her life, I was with her more than I had been my whole life.

We talked, prayed, laughed, and cried together. We told stories which we had never shared with one another, and shared the truth about our feelings. We acknowledged the accidental pain we had caused each other. She came to trust me. I bathed her and shared her last meal with her, sitting next to her on the side of her bed.

Her journey from this earth to heaven was a violent one, but we were able to bring peace to her by leaning on the source of love, God. Praying with her, holding her hand, listening to beautiful Christian music, praying the Rosary, which was wrapped around her cold, crippled hands, and sharing the Eucharist with her during her final days intimately connected us. During her last couple of weeks. I discovered firsthand the grace of forgiveness and mercy, which are essential components of lasting love.

No matter what, as long as we are breathing we can discover real love, gifted to us by God's grace...I had never thought of love as a decision to forgive: pretty powerful when one experiences it like I did!

Questions to ponder:

1. Were you ever wrong about a first impression? When you tried to put yourself in somebody else's shoes, did that change your mind about someone?

2. Did anyone ever give you another chance, a "do over?"

Pam Heil

Matthew 22: 37-39

You shall love the Lord, your God, with all your heart,
with all your soul, and with all your mind. This is the
greatest and the first commandment. The second is like
it: You shall love your neighbor as yourself.

(NABRE)

Chapter 5. Can the Greatest Commandment Really Help?

When Jesus was asked, "Which is the greatest commandment?" He replied, "Love the Lord your God with all your heart, with all your mind, and with all your strength, and love your neighbor as you love yourself."

As a child I didn't love myself. As an adolescent girl, I always felt less than beautiful, less than smart, less than good enough. I thought I could love God and others and not love myself.

As a young woman competing with the images of celebrity beauty, which were everywhere, I felt ugly. Even when I married, I was easily jealous during the first year of marriage and fearful when my husband travelled that he would find someone else. I did not love myself enough to believe that I was truly loveable.

Over the years, I discovered that anytime we compare ourselves to others, we would find someone better than we are. To find joy in ourselves, we should only compare ourselves with the person we were the day before to see if we are growing into the person God calls us to be.

If we are insecure or feeling inadequate, we are often destined to have unhealthy relationships with others. We become exceptionally needy, very demanding, and easily jealous.

If your best friend invites someone else to hang with you, you could feel threatened by his or her presence; you may fear that you will be replaced. If your boyfriend or girlfriend is talking to or laughing with someone else of the opposite gender, you may fear that he/she is cheating on you. Only when we feel loved and secure, can we feel safe in our relationships.

I came to discover how essential it is to truly love myself if I am going to truly love another. God made each of us good. Discovering our goodness and giftedness is necessary if we are going to be able to contribute love to our world in the way God calls each of us to do. I had trouble believing that I was good enough.

Recently, after a lifetime of feeling "less than", I took a huge step toward loving myself. My mom was a drop dead gorgeous woman, the one everybody's eyes turned toward when she entered a room. I did not look like my mom!

For a multitude of reasons, I never thought I was beautiful. I became legally blind when I was five, and wore very thick glasses. I had very curly hair, and all the pretty girls had beautiful straight hair. I loved sports before it was cool to be a female athlete, and didn't like jewelry or makeup, so I felt weirdly different.

I became a food addict. I was lucky because I loved to be active and to work out, but food controlled me. When I felt sad, or lonely, or less than whomever I thought I should be, as a sister, daughter, friend, wife, or mother, I stuffed my face with food.

Eventually, I became heavy, then obese, and then morbidly obese, which means my health was being compromised by my weight. I didn't want my picture taken. I began to feel like a failure as a wife and mother. I was embarrassed by my appearance, so I didn't buy new clothes because it was depressing to shop. I began to feel insecure, and I doubted myself.

Each day I vowed to begin eating in moderation, instead of binge eating. Each day about 3:00 in the afternoon I would begin to eat a crazy amount of food.

Some people crave sugar; some people crave salty foods. My curse was that I craved both. If I had salty first, I would rapidly follow with sweets. If I had sweets first, I would go for the chips or pretzels. I was out of control and getting more and more depressed.

I felt like a failure and a bit of a fake, because I was always talking about love in my speaking ministry.

Then, I found a program, which connected me with a person I could call anytime I needed to have an accountability partner. She helped to keep me on track; she listened to my feelings, and helped me set and accomplish goals. She is helping me conquer my addiction, one day at a time.

Whenever we are headed down a path, which is not bringing us the true joy God desires for us, we are lucky that our God built us for relationships. He put others in our lives to re-direct us.

Ask for and accept help. God can be a source of strength, for sure, but sometimes, we just need God with skin on.

Questions to ponder:

1. Do you ever have a tough time loving yourself? Are you your worst critic?

2. Do you need to find an accountability partner or someone to remind you of the gifts and talents that make you special? (I highly recommend that you find a Michelle in your life. She lives in Toronto. I have never met her, but she is helping me change my life, so I can more easily love myself!)

"The supreme happiness of life is the conviction that we are loved, loved for ourselves, or rather loved in spite of ourselves."

Victor Hugo

Chapter 6. Loving Me Is Not So Easy

You may be thinking, "Loving me is not so easy!" I am moody, unpredictable, and overly sensitive. Sometimes, I am demanding, bossy, and selfish. Sometimes, I get jealous and envious of others. I sometimes hold grudges, gossip, and become terribly impatient with others.

Sometimes, I am just not very nice!

How can we begin to love ourselves, even though we know we are not perfect, even though we know that others are better than we are at certain things, even though a friend or someone, whom we thought loved us, dumps us?

The answer comes from the first part of the greatest commandment: love God with all that we are: mind, body, and soul. To make that possible, we need to be in an intimate relationship with the source of love, God.

The closer we are to God, the easier it is to love. We can come to believe that God loves us, each of us, perfectly. Marriage Encounter, a retreat and lifestyle designed to enrich the lives of married couples, has a saying, "God doesn't make junk!"

If only we could believe that our God loves us unconditionally. If only we could know in our very core, that there is nothing that we can ever do that could make God love us less, and there is nothing we could ever do to make God love us more. God loves us as the beautiful people he created us to be.

Daily, we have to choose to become the best version of ourselves. Prayer and inspirational people can help us.

I have a friend whose son was brutally kidnapped and murdered by two young men in a completely random act of senseless violence.

Because the crimes were committed in two different states, there were numerous appeals after the two were first found guilty of kidnapping and murder. The two men never felt remorse and sat in the courtroom and smirked at my friend Rachel during each of the hearings.

I can only imagine how furious I would be. I have to admit I am still angry.

When I first heard Rachel tell her story of Brian's horrible death, she began with a request of her audience. "Would you please pray with me for Nathan and Terrell that someday we will embrace one another in heaven." After an emotional account of the tragedy and pain which she had endured and realizing that her pain was still raw and dreadful, she revealed to us that Nathan and Terrell were the two men who had chosen to kill her son, just to see what it would feel like.

My friend, who is a beautiful example of love and mercy in my life, chose to forgive instead of to hate those lost, empty souls who took joy in killing her son. As she listened to their lawyers' stories, she realized that these two had never felt loved in their lives, and thus, could not love another.

She opened up a center called Run the Race Club for children who are being raised in the same environments of emptiness: failing families, failing neighborhoods, and failing schools, as Nathan and Terrell were.

She chose to love unconditionally, like God loves us. I know the only way she can do this is because of her intimate relationship with her God. God is the source of true, unconditional love.

Questions to ponder:

1. Is it hard for you to fathom that you could be loved the same, no matter what you ever did or said?

2. Have you ever been given unearned forgiveness? How did you feel afterwards?

Pam Heil

Isaiah 41:10

Do not fear: I am with you; do not be anxious: I am your God.

(NABRE)

Chapter 7. Not So Sure I Even Believe in God

How can I come to love a God that I am not even sure exists? I have a story that may help answer this question.

When I was in San Antonio for a National Catholic Youth Ministers Conference, something totally unexpected happened. Several youth ministers and I had already showered and were in our pajamas when we discovered that Mary, a new youth minister from our diocese, was flying in late and hadn't eaten anything since lunch.

We wanted to make sure that she felt welcomed, so we decided to go down to the bar in the hotel to sit with her while she ordered food and ate some dinner. One of my friends had her leg resting on the arm of my chair. I started giving her a foot massage and while we all talked about our day, I probably massaged her foot for twenty minutes.

Two guys jumped up and excitedly came over to our table of women just chatting and laughing together. One guy came up to me and said, "That is the coolest thing I have ever seen. No way would you ever see dudes do what you ladies are doing!" He was referring to my giving my friend a foot massage. We just laughed and thought nothing of it.

The guys did not walk away. They looked a little mystified. One asked, "Who are you and why are you in San Antonio?"

We explained that we were all youth ministers, and we were there for a conference. He laughed as he exclaimed, "That explains a lot!"

He then asked the name of the conference we were attending, and when he found out we were Catholic, he said, "I think teenagers are messed up, and I don't believe in God!" His friend chimed in and declared that he too was an atheist.

I calmly said, "Really, tell me about the God you don't believe in." I listened as the one man told me how he could not make sense out of a God that allows injustices to occur and horrible tragedies like earthquakes and floods, and how a Church can allow priests to abuse children, and, and, and…

It seemed to me it was hard for him to understand why bad things happen to good people and how good things sometimes happen to bad people. This reality is a difficult concept for us humans to wrap our heads around.

The other gentlemen then told me about the God he did not believe in. He was abandoned as a child and adopted by a family who abused him. He ran away, took a few detours with decisions he had made about alcohol and other drugs, and became rather violent at times. There was definitely and internal rage which drove his sense of abandonment by any being, whom some would call GOD.

I listened with my ears and my heart. I heard their pain and disillusionment.

I then took a risk and asked them if they believed in LOVE. Each immediately said, "Yes!" I told them I believed what Scripture tells us that God is love. They then looked at me with an even more intense interest.

I asked them why they so quickly and easily said they believed in love. The one told me he has a teenager who he adores, but whom he worries about so much because of some of the decisions he was making. He keeps giving his son chance after chance to change and is always working to forgive him because he knows that inside his son is really a good and talented person. (Was he describing God and his relationship with each of us?)

This man was also a voracious reader of St. Augustine, St. Thomas Aquinas, and St. Ignatius. He was obviously a searcher and looking for proof of God's existence.

The other, the confirmed atheist, told me that he believed in love because of his marriage. He told me his wife loved him with all his imperfections, and that her unconditional love sometimes moved him to tears. He also spoke of his small children and how they ran into his arms each time he came home, and how much he was missing them while he was separated from them by the conference he was attending.

His description sounded to me like our God who loves us with all of our imperfections and who greatly misses us when we distance ourselves from him.

Each of us exists because of God's love, and it is because he loved us that we are capable of loving. First John tells us that! If we believe that, then we can only know a deeper love of self and others, if we grow closer to this God of ours, who is truly mystery.

Some may view God as a judge, keeping track of all our mistakes and accomplishments, so he can punish us or reward us. Some view God as Santa Claus: if I am good, he will give me awesome gifts and whatever I ask for. Some view God as a dictator: do this, don't do that. Some view God as a magician: he can make bad things disappear.

If we view God in any of these limited ways, it is no wonder that so many become so disillusioned by him, that belief in him disappears. God created us good. He created us free, free to choose. Sometimes, we choose things that are not good for us, or for others, and when we do, those decisions distance us from God, who is love. When we feel abandoned by God, or invisible and insignificant to Him, it is not because God moves away from us or rejects us, but because we begin to separate ourselves from God.

When we remove ourselves from God, we are not very nice. We may become extra impatient, extra critical of others, extra hard on ourselves, so much so that we become depressed because we feel isolated and alone.

Sometimes, others do things, which are selfish, and hurtful because of whatever love is missing from their lives, and they inflict pain on innocent people. Sometimes, people hate so much, that they massacre people who they deem different from themselves, or seem to take joy in killing innocent people. (We all know instances of evil and hatred in our world.)

Finally, sometimes, this wonderful world that is so symbiotically made gets out of whack because of something that goes awry in nature when natural disasters happen and thousands of people die.

The question that arises when all these things go wrong is "Where is God in all of this?"

Questions to ponder:

1. Is it hard for you to believe in God when the world seems to be spinning in crazy, cruel directions?

2. Can you receive comfort and confidence from the poem, "Footprints?" (Google it!)

Pam Heil

The Shack

"Remember this: humans are not defined by their limitations, but by the intentions that I, (Papa, God) have for them: not by what they seem to be, but by everything it means to be created in my image."

William Paul Young

Chapter 8. God Is With Us and in Us

God is with us and in us! "Footprints" is a great little poem reminding us that in the worst of times, God is lovingly carrying us. I also believe that God lives within us. If we see God in one another, we will be more forgiving, more patient, more present, and more loving toward one another.

God wanted us to have total peace, total joy, total beauty, and perfect love around us. The description of this heavenly place is depicted in the story of Adam and Eve in the Garden of Eden. Most know the story of the human greed and desire to know all and to be all.

God gave them guidelines as to how to live, but he loved humans enough to give us the freedom to choose. Each day, we can choose to be other-centered or self-centered. Each day we can choose to be satisfied or greedy. Each day we can choose to trust that God is all that we need, or we can search for peace, love, and joy in the transient things of this world.

St. Augustine wrote, "Our soul is restless, Lord, until it rests in you." I paraphrase this by saying, "There is a God-shaped hole in the heart of everyone of us that cannot be filled by anything else, if we are to experience the love, the joy, and the peace that God desires for us.

The question might be,"With what are your trying to fill that hole, which is making you feel sad, anxious, empty, or alone?"

The promise is that God will be with us in all of life, even when we don't notice because we are so self-absorbed in what we think is important, that we fail to recognize him. God is with us.

God is in us! One beautiful way to describe God is through the Trinity. Richard Rohr, a Franciscan priest suggests that we are intrinsically like the Trinity, living in absolute relatedness. We call this love. God is relationship; God is love!

Questions to ponder:

1. If you believed that the Spirit of God lives within you, would you treat yourself differently? Would you treat others differently if you believed the Spirit of God lives within them?

2. With what have you tried to fill the hole in your heart? Are there things that you are buying, doing, craving, or seeking that are not bringing you peace, joy, and love?

Pam Heil

In our busy world, we sometimes don't even know our next-door neighbors. Let us change that and move to a shared humanity, recognizing all whom we meet as NEIGHBOR!

Chapter 9. But Relationships Are Hard: Love My Neighbor?

Who's That?

I get that I am supposed to be in relationship. I know we live in a global world, and everyone is supposed to be my neighbor. But if you are like me, I have a hard time even liking some people. How can I obey the commandment to love my neighbor?

The good news is we don't have to like everyone. Nowhere does Jesus say we have to like everyone. You are probably thinking what most native English speakers think that love is just a stronger form of like.

St. Thomas Aquinas wrote, "To love is to will the good of another. "If you think about it, that means we have to desire what is good for everyone. That sounds like something that we can decide to do.

Psychologists realize that love is a decision. Ask anyone who has been in a long term, committed relationship, like marriage. Although each of us was created good, none of us is perfect. Therefore, each day I have the choice to focus on the good in another, or to focus on their imperfections. Each day I can choose to give someone a fresh start, or I can focus on something that irritated me the day before or even something that angered me or hurt me.

Holding grudges or holding on to anger or frustration truly zaps the energy out of a person. There is a saying, "Hatred hurts the hater. "I believe forgiveness is freeing, and it is truly necessary for peace within our hearts, or within our families, within our neighborhoods, and within our world.

There will always be pain in our world, but we can lessen that pain by choosing not to intentionally hurt anyone. We accidentally hurt people all of the time, so we don't need to do it on purpose.

Think about the times someone misinterpreted a text, or an Email. Think about the times when the words just came out of your mouth wrong, and you didn't really mean what you said. Think about the times you spoke before you thought and spewed out hateful, harsh, judgmental words onto someone you truly loved, just because you were "hangry" (hungry and thus angry or excessively irritable or sensitive).

Accidental pain happens and often leads to violence. I would like to share a different view of the fist, often thought of in terms of aggression or fighting. Make a fist and look at it right now. You have four knuckles protruding and each of these knuckles can depict for us a formula to bring healing and peace to troubled relationships.

The first knuckle will represent the word, "Please." When we say please, we are being polite and honoring the person's right to say, "No." When we don't say please and demand something of someone, we can easily be perceived as an aggressor, or a power figure instead of a companion or friend on the journey of life.

The second knuckle should remind us of two words, "Thank you." When we use this phrase we are showing appreciation for an act of service done for us, or for positive affirmations, or for something that fed us in some way. This phrase can affirm someone else's worth.

Many people feel invisible, insignificant, used, under-appreciated. Thank you's can work miracles in relational connectedness.

The third knuckle stands for three words, "I like you, or I love you." Words can build up, and they can tear down. Actually, hearing these words can truly stroke someone's inner-core.

These words, especially accompanied by actions, can bring joy to someone who is feeling down, can bring peace to someone who is struggling, can actually give someone a desire to live, to go forward, especially if they are feeling useless or hopeless. Researchers say, people would not commit suicide, if they truly felt loved, valued, or treasured by someone, only one person.

The fourth knuckle stands for four words: "Will you forgive me?" You probably had thought the words, "I am sorry," would have been somewhere in this strategy for healing relationships. Saying, "I am sorry," can really be an empty expression because it says nothing about the feelings of the other person.

Imagine two little toddlers fighting over the same toy, kicking, pushing, and maybe even biting. Mom comes in and pulls them apart, takes the toy, and sternly says, "You will not be allowed to play with each other until you say you are sorry." They are young, but fairly smart, so they say, "Sorry." They falsely think the word is magic cause they get to resume play.

Apologies are important; acknowledging when you are wrong is important, but asking for forgiveness acknowledges that you have wounded another, and healing takes time. Mercy and forgiveness are choices the victim will have the right to offer immediately, or over time.

After a period of time, hugs are also a powerful way to offer healing, but only if you ask the person, if you can hug them. Written notes of apology are so rare anymore that they are effective too… not just a text, but a heartfelt expression of sorrow or remorse, truly owning and expressing how you have hurt someone.

Communication is crucial to healthy relationships. Honesty is essential. Listening is validating. Clarifying what you hear is helpful, so you don't assume someone means something they really don't. The danger in communicating only through social media is the words are often limited, and the emotions are often inadequately expressed even with Emojis.

So, Who are our neighbors? Our neighbors are everyone with whom we come into contact. Being kind and polite to everyone is essential to building healthy relationships.

While shopping recently, I noticed a cashier being very unfriendly and short—tempered with the customer in front of me.

She was definitely in a foul mood. I read her body language and identified her non-verbals, because I looked at her. I wasn't on my phone, or texting; I noticed her.

While unloading my groceries onto the conveyor, I looked at her and smiled. I asked her if she was just starting her day or if her shift was about over, and I kindly told her I hoped her day would get better. She smiled and was completely transformed just by a smile and recognition of her emotions.

Another time, I was playing a very competitive tennis match against two very seasoned players, who my partner knew from her indoor leagues. My partner told me the one opponent was a real "B" and was notorious for making bad calls. I smiled and said, "Then, we will kill her with kindness." On each changeover, I handed her the balls, smiled, and said something funny about the previous games and myself. Pretty soon, on changeovers, she was handing me the balls and joking right back. Late in the third set, at a very crucial point she allowed us a replay because of a ball rolling behind her, which she was not required to do according to the rules.

Kindness begets kindness. It works most of the time, and all people have less tension and more fun.

Reading non-verbals, listening with our eyes and our hearts, not just our ears can help us be connected to all those whose paths we cross. The command to "Love your neighbor," is easier when you look at them, smile at them, and notice them. Kindness brings out the good in people. Love can build a bridge between their heart and yours.

Questions to ponder:

1.   1. What do you think of Thomas Aquinas's definition of love? Does it make you feel better to think you don't have to like everyone?

2.   Have you ever been nice to someone you didn't really like, and then you got to know them and you found out they were very likeable and you became friends? (Try it!)

"Love is what is in the room at Christmas if you stop opening presents and just listen."

Anonymous child

Chapter 10. The Simple Wisdom of Children about Love

There is a saying: "Out of the mouths of babes." This suggests that there is a truth, and innocent honesty with which kids speak. Many a parent has been embarrassed because a child has asked, "Why is that person so fat?" "What happened to that person's face?" "Why does that person have a metal leg?"

Kids are curious. They are honest, and they observe. That is how they learn. Below are some insights from children between the ages of 4-8. They were asked by a psychologist doing research to define love.

The question was simply, "What do you think love is?"

Their answers are listed below in quotations, with thoughts from me in parentheses.

"Love is that first feeling you feel before all the bad stuff gets in the way." (There is a saying that, "Love is blind," and in a way, it is. When we are first attracted to someone, we only notice the good in them.)

"When my grandmother got arthritis, she couldn't bend over to paint her toenails anymore. So my grandfather does it for her all the time, even when his hands got arthritis too. That's love." (Love is unselfish. It doesn't keep score. There is true joy in serving others, even if it hurts.)

"When someone loves you, the way they say your name is different. You know that your name is safe in their mouth." (So many times, we are wounded by the words of others. Those opinions are now often communicated without even looking at someone's face. When written, posted, texted, or tweeted, people can say hurtful things anonymously, and never see the pain their words could inflict.)

"Love is when a girl puts on perfume, and a boy puts on shaving cologne, and they go out and smell each other."

"Love is when you kiss all the time. Then, when you get tired of kissing, you still want to be together, and you talk more. Mommy and daddy are like that. They look gross when they kiss."

"When you tell someone something bad about yourself, and you are scared they won't love you anymore, but then you get surprised, because not only do they still love you, they love you even more." (That is real love.)

"Love is when you tell a guy you like his shirt, and then he wears it everyday." (It is really hard to let a person know you like them, like them. In today's world, our media tells us we are to talk a certain way, dress a certain way, act a certain way, and treat each other a certain way, and many of those suggestions will get us into trouble because they won't help us develop healthy relationships. How to flirt is not good advice. Just be yourself and respect and care for the other person, by listening to them, noticing them, and sharing time and interests with them.)

"During my piano recital, I was on stage, and I was scared. I looked out and saw all the people watching me, and I saw my daddy waving and smiling. He was the only one doing that. I wasn't scared anymore. That is love." (Remember, when your parents could kiss your booboo's and make them better. Maybe, life would be easier for you as you travel from childhood to adulthood if you trust your parents' love for you. Trust them with your troubles, struggles, and questions a little more.)

"I know my older sister loves me because she gives me all her old clothes and has to go out and buy new ones."

"I let my big sister pick on me because my mommy says she only picks on me because she loves me. So, I pick on my baby sister, because I love her."

"When you love somebody, your eyelashes go up and down and

little stars come out of you." (Sounds like a cartoon, huh? Guys have told me when they first fall in love, that it is scary, like an out of body experience. Why would they rather wait around at the possibility of seeing her, than shooting hoops with their buddies? Weird!)

"You really shouldn't say "I love you," unless you mean it, but if you mean it, you should say it a lot because people forget."

"God could have said magic words to make the nails fall off the cross, but he didn't. That is love."

If all these children seemed to get what love is, how did we forget? Why have we forgotten? Why are we confused? Puberty hits…"Yes." That is part of it, but also, as we get older, we have become surrounded by the media's influence, and we have become obsessed with sex. Bombarded with images of nudity, obscenities, and recreational sex, the world seems to have forgotten what real love is.

Questions to ponder:

1. Which child's definition of love made you go, "Awwww"?

2. Did any of these definitions make you teary-eyed, either with envy or nostalgia of a time in the past, which was simpler and easier?

Section II: The Struggle

"Don't advertise it if it ain't for sale."

Grandma's Quote

Chapter 11. Sex Sells

There are challenges and obstacles in our lives, which can cause us to move away from real love, to actually decrease our chances of finding it in our relationships. We are forced to make decisions at earlier and earlier ages about sex, alcohol, and other drugs, and if we get wounded or even trapped by these dangerous or destructive decisions, we can begin to doubt our very worth.

I am sure you have noticed that our world is permeated with sex. Sex is used in advertising to sell just about anything. I once heard advertisers on the radio trying to sell seats for an athletic event by having obvious moaning and groaning, simulating hot sex, for purchasing a hot seat before they sold out. Really?

Sex is used to define who we are, when our physical being is such a small part of who we are. I have a friend who was telling me about her new gay hair stylist, and I said, "How is he at cutting hair? I really don't care what he does in his bedroom."

We never used to define someone by his or her sexual preference. Seeing two guys at a movie theater sitting next to each other never used to cause someone to assume that they were gay. Women who played sports were called, "Tomboys" but people didn't classify female athletes as lesbians, just because they could throw, kick, or hit a ball, or shoot a basket. If two female teachers lived together for a lifetime, we didn't believe they had to be a couple; we just knew they were best friends.

How did we get to this obsession with the physical activity two people might engage in? When did this subject that used to be so private become so public? What can we do to bring the privacy back to something created to be special, private, and even sacred?

Humans are beautifully and wonderfully made. We are intellectual, social, which defines our emotional and relational side, spiritual, and physical beings. Yes, we are encased in a body, but that is merely our shell.

When Playboy or pornography first hit the scene, male defenders of this medium used to say, "What's wrong with it? Is there anything more beautiful than the human, (female) body?" My answer is, "Yes, the human person!"

The latest research I have found about pornography is an indicator of how dangerous this "harmless" journalism has become. Decency and restraint are disappearing. There are 300 million pornographic web pages on the Internet. Porn accessible mobile devices have now passed computers as the most common means of accessing porn with a quarter of a billion people using them in 2017 to access porn. Most porn is now free. It is now easily accessible, affordable, acceptable, (Surveys indicate that more people think it is immoral to not recycle than to watch porn.) It is anonymous (easily watched in privacy), aggressive (eroticizes the degradation of women and even children), and active (Self-producing and distributing porn is now easy) (Christian Counseling Today: Porn and Sex Addiction)

Porn affects kids relationally, emotionally, intellectually, neurologically, and spiritually. Meg Meeker writes that an 8 year old boy can find videos of sex between women and men, between women, between men, or both while innocently searching for something else on the Internet.

Traumatized by the images, but also hard to avoid because of curiosity, young people see sexually disturbing, confusing, and erotic activities. Teens who are porn observers often become sexually active and are at a higher risk for depression. Texting, sexting, and web cams are causing an evolution of the production of self-pornography.

Adults are also negatively affected by pornography. Neuroscience is proving that marital sexual problems, addictions to masturbation or self-gratification, and addiction to porn are real. My priest friend told me of the 11 couples who came to him with divorce requests in a year, 10 stemmed from weekly if not daily porn usage. Regular sex becomes boring for many because of regular pornographic exposure.

Have you heard enough about porn and the degradation of sex? Me too. But before we move on, let's take a look at language and dress.

Gentlemen and ladies possessed certain decorum before social media became available 24 hours a day. Women dressed modestly. (My grandma used to say, "Don't advertise it if it's not for sale!") A gentleman stood when a lady entered the room, removed his hat when he entered a building, and never spoke of or used language insulting to a lady.

Sometimes men used language in the locker room, which they would never have used in front of a lady. The "F" bomb would never have been used by a woman, and certainly would not have been used as a verb, an adjective, a noun, or an adverb, as it is commonly used in the media right now. Movies, which would have been considered X-rated a few years ago are now R and some even PG 13. For real!

You may be thinking, so what! Why are you writing about all that stuff? All of that is a thing of the past. You are talking about the old days. You are right: I am!

However, if I don't tell you how it used to be, you may not know that you have a choice to restore the respect that sex is due. Remember, you can't make something happen without believing it is possible, and change takes focus and effort.

Before sex became so public, people actually got married and stayed married. Children were born after marriage. Dads were actually a part of the family. People were aroused by the beauty of and desire for the opposite gender, but they didn't immediately act on those desires.

Yes, there was prostitution. There were the "Bad Boys" and the "tramps" as those who didn't follow the norms were called. There was some infidelity in marriage, but go ahead and Google the statistics on marriage and divorce over the last 40-50 years. Maybe, they were doing something right when divorce was rare, and kids knew who their fathers were.

The family needs to be restored. People need to have a place where they feel safe, secure, and loved. Children need to feel a sense of belonging, and a shared responsibility in contributing to family life. They need to experience mercy and unconditional love when they make mistakes or get temporarily trapped in the suffering caused by any decisions, which actually work against loving and respecting oneself and those around us.

We will work on a plan to help you create that kind of love and family in your life in Section III, but for now, let's examine your attitude about sex.

Questions to ponder:

1. Would you like a person to love you for who you are instead of how your body makes their body feel?

2. Do you find yourself thinking about sex all the time? What can you do to restore the sacredness of sex?

The misuse of sex is negatively affecting family. Recreational sex is hurting our relationships and causing a great deal of confusion about love.

Chapter 12. My Views on Sex

Sex was God's idea! In Genesis, in the creation stories, we were told, "It was good," after each of God's creations. Adam and Eve were naked and not ashamed because the body had done no evil. They were told to be fruitful and to multiply. A man was to leave his father and mother and be joined to his wife, and they shall become one flesh.

In the Book of Solomon it is apparent God gave us each other for passion and pleasure in marriage. In Hebrews, it is written that marriage should be held in honor among all.

Sexuality is all that makes us human: mind, body, soul, and spirit. We are so much more than just or bodies, our gender, or our choices about how we try to bring pleasure to our body or the body of another.

Theology of the Body is a view of sex and sexuality, which can conquer some of the negative affects of pornography, and sexual promiscuity in our society. This theology stemmed from hundreds of letters written by Pope John Paul II during his tenure as pope. This pope loved teenagers and young adults and gathered them together regularly for World Youth Day.

I was privileged to attend a World Youth Day in Toronto. The Pope had been victimized by advanced stages of Parkinson Disease late in his ministry., and there was a rumor stirring about amongst the masses that because of his compromised health, JPII might not have been able to make the trip from Rome. The masses of people were told that for sure, he would not be able to officiate at Mass, that he would definitely not be able to distribute the Eucharist, and he would not be giving the homily. We were also warned that he would not be able to smile and would probably not be able to speak because of the paralysis of his facial muscles.

One million people, most of them young, were eagerly waiting for the sighting of the helicopter, which would be delivering the pope. The crowds were in a frenzy as they began chanting, "JPII, we love you," and "Papa" and other terms of affection, when they viewed the Pope disembarking onto the helipad.

As he was assisted into the Pope-mobile, I had goose bumps, and I was moved to tears by the intense joy that enveloped the Pope's face. He was smiling and waving to the crowds of young people. His body was driven by the love he felt for us, and his facial muscles were functioning because he wanted us to feel his love and respect for us. From the stage onto which he was lifted, the microphone was placed in front of him and with a booming voice he greeted us, "My dear young friends!" It was amazing and awesome. The crowd erupted in a multitude of languages with expressions of their love for John Paul II. The prayers and the genuine love of the million people restored his strength, and he was able to celebrate Mass, give the homily, and distribute Communion.

I told you all of this to assure you that this man loved you and believed in you and wanted you to experience the peace, love, and joy that God desires for each of us to have: not just in the next life, but now. He spoke of the pain, the brokenness, and the sadness that he had been viewing in the faces of young people in recent years, and how sad it made him to see their pain.

He attributed the sorrow, loneliness, depression, and even suicide, which were becoming rampant, to a disregard for the sacredness of the body. I agree with him.

As a youth minister who has listened and supported teenagers, young adults, and their parents on their journeys through life, I have come to believe that most of the problems in life are connected to our disconnect in relationships. We are all searching for love, for significance, for appreciation, and for joy, and we have come to believe that whatever gives us a few moments of pleasure will assist us in our quest for happiness.

Our media has depicted sex as intensely pleasurable, loud, long lasting, multi orgasmic, cure-all for all that ails us.

I once had a junior in high school who had come into my office each morning for a week with nausea. I comforted her each day and talked with her about issues in her life, which might have upset her stomach. She was missing a father figure, and didn't understand guys, but she wanted a boy to love her. She was having a tough time focusing on school, and all she wanted to do was sleep.

After the third day, I asked this straight A, honor roll student if she was sexually active, and she vehemently told me no, and that she was a virgin. I asked her if she had been to a doctor about her nausea and exhaustion, and she announced that they had no medical insurance, so her mom told her basically to suck it up.

On the 5th day, I asked her if she might be pregnant, and she started crying. As I held her, she said she was afraid. After a little more time, I asked her if she had a boyfriend. She said she had dated a senior a couple of times, but he wasn't really a boyfriend. I asked her gently what they had done on their dates. She told me, and her answers led me to my next question, "Did you have sex?" She proclaimed her virginity again.

The next day she was back in my office, looking exhausted and drained, vomiting yet again. My motherly instinct was kicking in, and I truly believed she was pregnant. Eventually, I asked, "When you were kissing this boy, did you have your clothes on?" She sheepishly answered, "No."

After some gentle prodding, in fact, I did discover that she did have sex with the boy, even though she didn't believe that she had, and she was pregnant! Her words were, "But it didn't feel wonderful; I didn't feel loved, it didn't last long, there wasn't moaning and pleasure, and I felt terrible afterwards. I thought I was still a virgin, honest."

Your education about sex cannot only come from the media, if you want to find out what making love is and if you want to discover what authentic, real love is. All animals can have sex, but only humans can make love, and many don't understand the difference.

Questions to ponder:

1. What is one message you repeatedly seem to hear in the media?

2. Are you countercultural in your views toward sex? That means do you disagree with the messages about, "If it feels good, do it!"

Beyond the Birds and the Bees

"Chastity is an empowering virtue that helps us to love the right person, in the right way, at the right time."

Greg and Lisa Popcak

Chapter 13. The Dating Game

Many of us will be called to the vocation of marriage and family. Even though many are choosing not to marry and are living together out of fear of commitment or divorce, when asked what they desired for their future, the most frequent answer is, "I would love to be happily married and have a wonderful, loving family." Yet, it is easy to make choices, which absolutely work against you in fulfilling this dream. Dating is a means by which you could find a mate over time.

Dating is a relatively new phenomenon, only about a hundred years old. Dating became recreational with the invention of the car. Courtship before that was in the presence of family. For centuries in many parts of the world, marriages were pre-arranged by culture, social status, ethnicity, tribal affiliation, family friendships, or religion. Even in our country where arranged marriages have been very rare, dating has changed.

Dating began as a fun way to get to know things about the opposite gender, while also growing in an understanding about yourself, and who you are. Because we are relational beings, dating is supposed to be fun, social, and a way to find a mate.

Ideally, with each dating relationship, you will become a better person, more aware of what it means and what it takes to be in a healthy relationship. You should become more aware of the give and take and the mercy and forgiveness necessary in a relationship, growing in feelings of trust, safety, and security.

Dating should help you laugh at yourself as you grow in knowledge of each other and develop a patience and consideration of one another. There should be an increased positive energy as you grow in personal confidence, which allows you to take off your masks and be vulnerably honest with one another about thoughts, feeling, dreams, fears, values, and beliefs.

In a healthy dating relationship, individuals help one another grow into the best version of themselves.

This growth process requires time, mutual effort, and trust. Sharing who you are with a date allows you to be honest in relaxed ways and to grow in thoughtfulness and consideration of the other persons' goals and objectives in life. When a dating relationship is healthy, the couple should also strengthen their relationships with others.

Dating can sometimes create an unhealthy relationship, because strong feelings can occur quickly and fade quickly. When jealousy and suspicion replace trust and confidence, there is an impatience and lack of consideration for the other because "it is all about me." In an unhealthy relationship the concern for physical appearances, popularity, and gratification of sexual desires replace getting to know each other, respecting each other's values and dreams, and celebrating the individuality of each person.

Decisions are forced onto one another in an unhealthy relationship, and sometimes other relationships suffer because of all the pressure on an individual. Often lying about where you are going or where you have been is a deterrent to maintaining a trusting relationship between the couple and their parents. Perhaps, one person's desire to take it slow in the physical activity department is not respected, and sometimes ultimatums are even given: "If you won't do such and such with me, I am out of here. There are plenty of other girls or guys who will."

When dating becomes intense and controlling or when individuals deal with one another in a possessive, restrictive manner, it is probably time to slow things down, to make some space, to take some time to evaluate if you are growing or wilting as a result of this particular dating relationship.

Sexual decisions often surface as the main catalyst for tough dating situations. Sex is a progressive activity. It might take a few weeks to first ask a girl or a guy out. Maybe, it will take a few dates to hold hands, a few more to kiss, a few more to French kiss, a few more to touch each other in erotic ways with clothes on, then a little while longer with clothes off… get the picture?

Because 61% of teen dating relationships end in 3 months and 80% end in 6 months, the next date's sexual activities could start with taking clothes off in a very short period of time. It is easy to take up wherever you left off in the previous dating relationship. Someone holding hands and kissing at the age of 11-12 has a 91% chance of intercourse by 18 years old. If a couple begins holding hands and kissing at 16, there is only a 20% chance of intercourse by 18. (<u>Christian Counseling Today</u>, 2015, Volume 21, No.1, American Association of Christian Counselors. Inc.)

There are true benefits to waiting until the age of 16 to date. If you date in 7th grade, only 29% of boys and 10% of girls are virgins when they graduate from high school. If you wait until 16 to date, 84% of boys and 82% of girls will be virgins when they graduate.

There are also physical risks for adding sex to dating. Two out of three AIDS carriers do not know they are infected because they can't tell; they can't see the symptoms. It takes an average of 10 years before you become sick from the HIV infection, and you can be contagious the whole time. The Aids virus is 450 times smaller that a sperm, and if 18.4% of girls under 18 get pregnant with a condom, it is kind of like a basketball lying on a football field. Besides AIDS, other sexually transmitted diseases are being spread orally, anally, and genitally.

Plus, you cannot put a condom on your heart. Emotional pain is real and difficult to heal when sex is added to a dating relationship. If you want what is best for you or someone else, you will not have sex in high school. You cannot promise forever with your body and a oneness with another, when you are not ready to have your own home, buy your own groceries, and pay your own bills. Bringing the you, who has attained goals, achieved some dreams, and knows oneself, into a relationship increases your chances of transforming a dating relationship into a happy, loving marriage.

For many teens there is a total disconnect between sex and love. In some schools, teens don't even date anymore. They just hook up, do Netflix and chill, seek friends with benefits or whatever the latest name is for having sex without any emotional attachment. This is another whole level of heartbreak for me, because sex is a beautiful expression of love, designed to be unitive and procreative for humans, not just a means to attempt to satisfy an animalistic desire.

Because we are not just animals, but rather human beings, we are capable of making love. We are capable of deciding to love another, capable of choosing to forgive another, capable of focusing on the good in another, and able to overlook imperfections, which exist in everyone.

We are capable of making love with another, being more concerned about bringing the other joy and pleasure, healing from any brokenness through the connectedness, so intimate that marital love is compared to Christ's love for his church.

The ideal is that making love would be sacred for a married couple because it allows them to be co-creators of life with God. In this intimate love relationship, two bodies join together to become one body, two people become one person, committed to each other for life. That is the ideal that God desires for us to have: ultimate pleasure, the deepest of intimacy, complete trust and vulnerability, and joy on this earth. All other sex may be orgasmic, but it is not special, sacred, treasured, and an expression of authentic love, which God desires for it to be. Why settle?

Having sex does not make you a robot; you can always choose to stop! You can choose to restore sex to the beautiful, sacred expression of love and commitment it was designed to be.

Questions to ponder:

1. In your world what does it mean to you to date someone?

2. Is sex assumed after a particular time of dating?

The Trinitarian God depicts God as three persons in one God. God the Father, who loves the son, Jesus; the son loving the Father, and the love between them, shared with all of humanity, is the Spirit. We are all called to that intimate, loving relationship with God and with one another.

Chapter 14. My Thoughts About Love

Gen. 2:18 "It is not good that man should be alone." We all need examples of marriages filled with grace, goodness, and happiness, or we may doubt that it is worth the energy and effort to strive for such a love.

Occasionally, there is a story of inspired love in a book or a movie. Last night I watched the movie, <u>The Longest Ride</u>. What a great love story! Rent it, if you can. It is the story of Ira and Ruth, a couple who fell in love before WWII when Ruth escaped Nazi extermination in Poland to emigrate to the U.S. After dating for a few months, Ira was going to ask her to marry him. Before Ruth said, "Yes," to Ira's proposal, she announced that she wanted many children. That was no problem for Ira.

They were truly joy-filled, but when the war erupted, Ira answered the call to serve and promised Ruth he would return to her. He was a hero in the war and while saving another's life he sustained injuries that would affect his life forever. Unselfishly, he tried to avoid Ruth because he was not the same man who had left her, and he would not be able to father children. She convinced him that she still loved him, they married, and theirs was a journey of real love.

The extra beauty in the story is how letters, which Ira had written daily to Ruth, were discovered by a young modern day couple. The depth of unselfish commitment, love, honor, and respect modeled through these letters further inspired and affirmed the young couple's desire to share that kind of love someday.

There are other movies, which convey the power of love to shape people into the best version of themselves like <u>A Walk to Remember</u>, and <u>The Notebook</u>. Even though there are aspects of their physical love that are vividly described, in a Hollywood kind of way, the characters are adults who are tender, unselfish, and committed, and the long term example of their marital love is beautiful.

Finding examples of real love in our world may be a challenge for you. If you have been victimized by abuse, divorce, betrayal, infidelity, assault, or rape, it may be very difficult for you to believe in love and thus, difficult for you to believe in God, who Scripture tells us is LOVE.

Trusting love is sometimes difficult. We wear masks to hide our imperfections if we are afraid that we have to look a certain way, act a certain way, or attain a certain level of success, in order to be worthy of love.

I believe that all people desire love and want loving relationships in their life, but we can only love to the degree that we know love. Therefore, some people are nasty, judgmental, aggressive, or down right mean because they are like an empty shell deprived of the pearl of love that allows humans to see beauty and possibility in life.

Without hope, which comes from the belief that people are innately good, or that bad things in life will be temporary, life is even tougher. I have found that hopeless people can be transformed by a consistent, positive relationship with someone who inspires them to discover their own gifts and talents or to nurture their own goodness.

To find the joy in real love involves a bit of a risk for sure. Some people for reasons of their own won't love us the way we need. Some people do not understand what commitment is, what honor is, or what integrity is. They have never witnessed it and have never learned it, so how could they trust others enough to get close enough to be hurt by them. To be vulnerable is difficult, but worth it when true love is found.

In your search for authentic love, hope will grow in you when you surround yourself with friends who build you up, challenge you, and support you on your journey. Find people with like values who help you make good choices even when bad choices are easily available. Find friends who can help you survive the tough times in life, because there will be tough times.

The following story will demonstrate how even a pain unimaginable to most of us becomes bearable when shared.

Jess was somewhat volatile. After I befriended her, she trusted me enough to share her story. She was a survivor. Not in the sense that she was just tough and resilient, but in the literal sense of the word.

Her father had been a violent, abusive alcoholic. When she was nine, her mother frantically awakened her sister and her in the middle of the night to flee their home to escape another one of his outbursts.

When they arrived at her aunt's house, she felt safe and went to sleep on a bedroom floor. She was awakened by gunshots. She crept down the stairs and saw her aunt lying dead on the floor and her father headed toward the stairs.

Hysterically but quietly, she retreated to her bedroom and tried to shelter her little sister as she heard screams and more shots. Then, her father burst into the room and shot her sister and her. As she lay in a pool of blood, faking her death, she watched her father shoot himself. She was the only survivor. Her father had killed her aunt, her mom, her cousin, her sister, and himself, and she wore the scar of a bullet hole in her neck.

Her emotional scars were more difficult to overcome than her physical wounds. Although nothing could change her past, she telling me her story was a first step to her healing. She trusted me to care and support her as she strived for peace and searched for love.

Although most of us may never have to endure Jess' kind of heartache, when pain strikes us, it hurts us deeply and it can consume us. We might even think something is so heavy that it is not survivable.

When we feel this way, we must reach out to others. We are created for intimacy, which is a closeness, a connectedness that is so deep that we are willing to share joys, sorrows, challenges, fears, and any aspect of our life with others because we value them, trust them, and respect them.

We must love ourselves enough to share our lives with others, and we must be people who are trustworthy, kind, and loving enough to be worthy of that trust and respect from another.

Questions to ponder:

1. How do you feel about the friends you have right now? Do your friends ask you to lie for them or to cover for them? You might want to consider changing friends.

2. Who has taught you the most about love? Who models love the most for you?

"No man is an island."

John Donne

Chapter 15. I Only Want What Is Good for You

We were not meant to be alone. If we take a look at life, each of us is born dependent. We need someone to feed us, to change our diapers, to protect us, and to provide for our basic needs. Then, as we approach adolescence, more than anything we want independence: we crave freedom.

As we mature, we come to realize that we were created to be interdependent. None of us is perfect. None of us can do everything by ourselves. We all have strengths and weaknesses. That reality calls us to relationship. My strengths can fill your weaknesses, and your strengths can fill my voids and inadequacies.

Loving relationships can complete us and empower us, but what is real love? Love is a word we use freely: "I love that dress," I love that movie," I love that song," I love chocolate." The meaning of this word is so abstract and so deep that we need to re-examine it. The ability to love is uniquely human. Although we all know that we are in the animal species, we are the only species capable of loving. Pet owners, who have a special relationship with their pets may argue, but we must know that a pet's attachment to us is not a conscious choice.

Humans are different; we can choose to love. Definitions and descriptions of love are everywhere. Books, songs, poetry, and movies try so hard to capture the depth of the meaning of love.

When I was a child, each time I went to church, I read above the altar, "No greater love than this, that a man lay down his life for a friend." I knew I couldn't argue that, but if I was called to love, could I ever give my life for another, and is that required of love?

"Love is patient. Love is kind. Love is not boastful…" wow!

Could I ever love like that? "Love your neighbor as you love yourself." But I didn't like myself; I was ugly. Did that mean I couldn't love another? Figuring out love is tough!

"To love is to will the good of another:" I felt that I was onto something in this simplistically profound statement. If I didn't wish evil on anyone and didn't hurt them on purpose, did that capture what love is?

During my time as a facilitator for support groups for international students, I realized the fine innuendos of language. In many languages an ending totally changes the meaning of the word. In English, for sure, there doesn't seem to be the perfect word to describe what we mean or feel. For example, does love mean a strong like? My students used to tell me that when they tried to buy a card for Valentine's Day for somebody special it was a real struggle to be completely honest. "I don't love him yet, but what I feel is stronger than like." "I don't want to give her the wrong impression by sending her a card filled with words of love, but she is more special than just a friend." Words are very powerful, and finding the right words to use, and using them honestly is important to our relationships.

I've come to believe that the words like and love are very different. The great commandment of love finally makes sense to me. I hope the following, helps you understand one way of looking at our call to love, and what that means.

God didn't command us to like one another. We have nothing in common with some people, so we just don't have fun with them. Some people are just not very likable. We aren't compatible with everyone, and some peoples' quirks and idiosyncrasies just irritate the heck out of us. Some people we just don't enjoy being around.

Despite the reality that you just don't like some people, you can still love them. Love is a conscious choice to do nothing to hurt another on purpose, and to wish them no harm. Now, does loving God, your neighbor, and yourself feel more doable to you?

Loving merely means not adding to the unavoidable, accidental pain that comes in all relationships. Loving in the Thomas Aquinas definition merely means respecting one another, being kind to one another, and never intentionally hurting someone. It means celebrating their successes and joys, and wanting what is good for them.

The "Love Your Neighbor" part of the Greatest Commandment, is, hopefully, clearer to you now. The being in love part is probably still a mystery. Let me tell you another story that will show you how confusing romantic love can be and how we can both send and receive false messages about what it really is.

I was at a rally giving a talk on love to about 400 high school youth. The night before, I had observed a couple at a dance, who I believed were in a deep relationship because of the way they were looking at each other, and because of the way they were dancing.

During my presentation, I asked them to come to the stage for a demonstration, and after talking with them briefly, I was shocked to discover that they had just met that day. Their body language certainly had suggested otherwise.

By touching and groping each other on the dance floor, the desire for sex seemed pretty intense. The PDA, the public display of affection, the public display of animalistic desire, was certainly different than the idea of sex as a sacred gift. I doubt that after one night, this young couple's physical contact was headed toward the unity that comes from loving another human being in an intimate, unconditional, committed way.

This young couple may have had religious convictions to wait until marriage, because they came to my workshop on chastity and love, but actions speak louder than words, and their actions were working against them.

Questions to ponder:

1. What are your actions saying about you? Are you sending false messages with your body?

2. Do you think there should be a relationship between sex and love? I suggest that you might love yourself enough to investigate what real/ authentic love is and to strive for it in your life.

"If you don't stand for something, you will fall for anything."

Anonymous

Chapter 16. You Have to Choose!

You have to choose what physical activities coincide with your sexual morality, because the sex drive is very powerful. I am going to present three moralities from which you can choose: Recreational, Relational, and Committal. You have to choose one code in order to have power over your decisions.

Your decisions can bring you heartache and pain, or a less stressful life, and an understanding of what real love is.

There is a great deal of sadness in our world because people are falling for the media's lies that suggest sex, alcohol, and drugs will bring you happiness, popularity, and an escape from the pain in life. Some even believe that sex will bring them love.

In the media, love is often depicted as one gland calling to another. I think you are hot; you think I am hot, so we are soon tearing each others clothes off and having sex on the floor, on the kitchen counter, in the backseat of the car, or maybe, even in a bed. Are we smart to believe in this kind of love? Maybe, when two people who are "hot" to one another, get physical, they will just get burned.

When you were young, parents or caregivers kept you from getting burned. I can bet that as a toddler, you didn't crawl into a fireplace when the fire was lit even though you thought it was really pretty. I'm sure most of you learned early not to ride your tricycles out in front of a moving car. I am sure some of you might have wanted to be a Super Hero and tried to fly out of a second story window. People, who love you, have said more than once, during your life: "No, no, no, that will hurt you. No, no, no!" <u>No</u> was a word used by people who loved you to protect you. <u>No</u> is a love word!

Because you are often in situations without an adult to protect you, you must decide when something is good or bad, when something is safe or dangerous, when something is right or wrong. You must decide when to say No, and you must love yourself enough to say, "No, no, no, that will hurt me. No, no no."

Morality is a code of right and wrong: it is what you determine to be good or bad. It is your core value system. In order to lead a life in which you are in control of who you become, you must determine for yourself what standards you will live by. Otherwise, anything and anyone could have control over you.

Each of you needs to determine for yourself a personal morality by which you will live, a basic code of right and wrong. Ideally, your chosen code will be good for you and will not hurt others. Different factors contribute to our deciding what we believe in, what we stand for.

One powerful contributing factor, which can influence who we become is the media. Human beings are part of the animal kingdom. As such, we share the instinct to survive, which means we sleep, eat, drink and have sex. Like animals, we are created male and female, two anatomically different bodies which allow one body to enter into another to create life. Recently, the media has not spent much time differentiating humans from animals because of the depiction of sex as nothing more than an act of sensual pleasure.

Repeatedly, the media uses music videos, movies, television, and computer pornography to promote sex as merely recreational and animalistic. Lyrics describe sex as hot and steamy, intense, temporary, immediate, impersonal, and at times, even violent. Foreplay can be people swearing at each other, pushing each other, tying each other up, and hitting each other prior to ripping each other's clothes off in a frenzy to have sex.

The media's description of sex is causing some real confusion about gender roles, flirting, dating, and how to relate to the opposite sex. Sex is depicted as a game, a way to dominate or control another, a way to get a guy or girl, a way to be popular, and sometimes, a way to find love and acceptance.

Younger and younger kids are imitating behaviors they see or hear about: oral sex and now even anal sex are becoming common among young teens. "Hooking up" and "friends with benefits" are evidence of a growing attitude towards sex, which I call a recreational morality: "Sex is fun; sex is free; sex is always for me! How can something which feels so good ever be bad?"

Sexual exploitation is causing a great deal of pain in young peoples' lives: not only are they being exposed to the possibility of an unwanted pregnancy, but also to numerous sexually transmitted diseases, an increase in cervical cancer, future sterility concerns, AIDS, and even human trafficking. The loss of love and respect for self is perhaps the worst consequence of a recreational morality. You cannot put a condom on your heart!

Questions to ponder:

1. Is it time for you to define for yourself what your personal morality regarding sex is? Do you believe there is anything to truly gain by having a recreational morality?

2. Do you think it is too late for you? I say, "It is never too late!" Today is a new day. You can choose to change.

The Road Less Traveled

"Two roads diverged in a wood and I- I took the one less traveled by, and that has made all the difference."

Robert Frost

Chapter 17. Should My Values
Hurt Me?

Your code of right or wrong, and good or bad is shaped by many things. Your faith, your family, and your friends, can all greatly impact your decisions. You need to have a foundation of personal beliefs to empower yourself and to protect yourself. Your personal morality will affect how you love, how you view sex, and when sex and love might best fit together, so each can be what God intended them to be.

If you have sex with lots of people, even if you get lucky and never get pregnant or get somebody pregnant, even if you never get a sexually transmitted disease, even if you avoid AIDS, you will be affected. The following story is an example of how devastating a recreational morality can be.

She was a 13-year-old freshman, new to our school. She knocked on my door and said, "Hey, I heard you were good to talk to. Can we talk?"

I said, "Sure, have a seat."

She began, "First of all, my life is good."

I realized that I hadn't heard that much from teenagers over the years, so I intently continued to listen with a great deal of curiosity. Her face did not convey joy or even happiness.

She continued, "Well, I might as well tell you like it is. I started smoking cigarettes when I was nine, drinking booze when I was 11, and smoking weed when I was 12. I've had sex with about six different guys, and right now, I am in love with a 23-year-old guy I met at the mall. Sometimes, I sneak out in the middle of the night, and we have sex in his car. My life is good."

I asked her if her life was so good, what did she need my help with?

I was saddened by her story, but I didn't react; I just listened with my heart.

Her tone changed to one of a somber concern, as she said, "I am worried about my kid sister."

I immediately assumed her younger sister was sick, but when I asked, that wasn't the issue. She shared a conversation with her sister from the night before where her 11-year-old sister told her she had been to a party and drank a lot of beer, and made out with a bunch of different guys over the weekend.

I replied, "So, why are you worried about her?"

She totally spazzed as she questioned how anybody could have assumed that I would be somebody to go to for help with a problem. Frustrated, she got ready to leave my office, shouting, "You just don't get it!" Are you crazy? My 11 year old sister is drinking and hooking up with a bunch of different guys, and you ask me why I am worried about her!"

I calmly and gently told her that I didn't get it, and asked her if she would please talk to me a bit more about her concerns for her sister, so I could understand.

I reminded her that she had just shared with me that she had been drinking, smoking, using drugs, and hooking up with guys for years, and she had said that her life was great. I told her I thought her little sister was just following in her footsteps and asked why she didn't want her sister to live her life the way she was living hers.

She tearfully, replied, "Because, I love my little sister."

I don't know if that freshman girl became a statistic because she moved away shortly after our conversation. I don't know if she became pregnant. I don't know if she contracted AIDS or some other sexually transmitted disease. I don't know if she ended up in a future abusive relationship with some older man. I don't know if she is living on welfare. I don't even know if she is still alive, but I do know that she no longer loved herself.

As a 13 year-old girl, she was settling for the life that her choices had created for her, but she didn't want the same life for her sister, because she loved her sister. It is a terrible tragedy when people no longer love and respect themselves because they have given up on finding love or being loved, something we are all deserving of.

Whatever morality you choose for yourself there will be physical, emotional, relational, and spiritual consequences. Think hard about what you believe in, and what your core values are. Remember, if you don't stand for something, you will fall for anything, but if you determine what you believe in, and what your core values are, you will be empowered.

Questions to ponder:

1. Do you think the choices you make affect others?

2. If I suggest that you love the world enough to think before you act, do you understand that I believe that we are all affected by the choices of others? Life is a series of ripple affects!

"Love is friendship that has caught on fire. It is quiet understanding, mutual confidence, sharing, and forgiving. It is loyalty through good and bad times. It settles for less than perfection and makes allowances for human weaknesses."

Ann Landers

Chapter 18. Another Choice for a Personal Morality Based on Love

Either because you have been raised in a church which teaches abstinence or chastity, or because you have had parents talk with you about the beauty of married love, or because you actually believe the health teachers when they talk about the dangers of sex, many of you may find it easy to reject a recreational morality. It may be easy for you to understand that a recreational morality minimizes both who you are and the sacredness of sex, and puts you at great risk for physical, emotional, or spiritual pain.

But what if you love someone? A relational morality basically states, "If I love someone, sex is a beautiful expression of love, and therefore, cannot be wrong." The difficult part about choosing a relational morality is basing your decisions about what to do with your body on the ambiguous meaning of love.

Again, the question is, "How do I know what love is? How do I know if what I am feeling is the real thing?" Will sex be all that it can be, and really great for me, and bring me wonderful feelings of being loved, if it doesn't last…even if I believed, I was in love?"

The first time I thought I was in love, I was in eighth grade. I can honestly say that I don't remember anything I learned in eighth grade, (a painful fact to me because I once taught eighth grade for three years), but I did think I had died and gone to heaven. Why? Because I was a somewhat ugly girl who got to look at the most gorgeous guy sitting in front of her all day. His name was Bill, and he was so cute!

Every single day, Bill walked me home from school, and carried my books. We talked about everything. I trusted him with every aspect of my life: trouble with friends, fights with parents, dreams, hopes, and fears. He always seemed to understand. He always seemed to appreciate me. We were so comfortable together. Life was just more fun when we were together, but when things were tough, they were always easier, when I shared my struggles with Bill. He was my best friend and his eyes and his smile made me melt.

Although Bill was gorgeous, the only word I could possibly use to describe me at that time was ugly. I had big puffed out curly hair when everyone else had beautiful straight hair. I wore thick cat eyeglasses because I was legally blind.

My glasses were so thick that I had no idea that I had beautiful blue eyes because when I had my glasses on I couldn't see my eyes because of the magnification of the lenses (not like today's featherweight lenses), and when I took my glasses off, I didn't know I had beautiful blue eyes, because I couldn't see my eyes.

I now realize that my inability to recognize anything beautiful about myself is a common phenomenon of the teenage years. You may never feel good enough, smart enough, beautiful enough, athletic enough, talented enough, or strong enough.

When we are young we never seem to feel that where we are is where we want to be, or how we want to be. No matter how old we are, we need to feel valued, appreciated, and loved to be totally happy about who we are. When something or someone helps us feel that way, it is awesome!

When I was with Bill, I felt beautiful. He treated me like a princess. He cared about me and wanted to be with me. He treated me so nice all the time, even when his buddies were around. (I noticed that sometimes boyfriends don't even talk to their girlfriends when they are around their guy friends.) I knew that what I felt toward Bill had to be love. I could never imagine feeling any closer to anyone.

The day after our 8th eighth grade graduation, my phone rang, and when I picked up, someone was crying on the other end. It was Bill. When I asked him what was wrong he told me he couldn't tell me on the phone. He asked if we could meet somewhere. I asked my mom. She said, "Yes."

Bill and I met two blocks away from my house at East Elementary School behind the swing sets. When I saw him he looked horrible; puffy eyes and blotches all over his face showed me that he had been crying a long time. I was scared.

He told me the saddest news that I had heard up to that time in my life. He told me he was moving and that this would be the last time we would be able to see each other. He was moving that week. His parents had waited to tell him that his dad was being transferred because they didn't want to ruin the end of his eighth-grade year.

I was shocked. I couldn't imagine not having Bill around. He was the love of my life. He was my best friend. He made me feel beautiful and special. I burst into tears, and we held each other in our arms as we both violently wept.

After a while, we began to talk. He told me he loved me, and I told him the same. He said he wanted to show me how much he loved me. I wanted to be closer to him than I had ever been. I wanted our last day together to be special.

So the first time I ever did it was with Bill, after my eighth grade, behind the swing sets at East Elementary School. I loved him, and he loved me, and it just seemed like the next step. We wanted to prove the depth of our love for each other.

So, why am I telling you about the first time I did it? Because, what Bill and I did to show how much we loved each other was kiss. What did you think we did?

I can guarantee you that you will never feel any emotion stronger than what I felt for Bill at that time in my life. He made me feel all warm inside, tingly all over, when he smiled at me, or when he held my hand. I wanted to be with him all the time. The difference is when I felt turned on and so close to Bill, and when he felt the same way toward me, we had not been told that it was okay to have sex. We were told if you loved and honored someone, you waited until marriage.

When Bill moved away, it was difficult and I was sad. I lost a great friend, and my first real boyfriend. I loved him in a very special way, but over the years there were other guys I thought I loved, and because I didn't add sex to those relationships, when I married my husband we shared something special.

One of the saddest things to me about young people today is for many, even the beauty of the kiss has been lost. Often, I hear of kids kissing and making out with just about everyone they meet. Then, when they really feel that they love someone, they automatically jump to sex as a way of showing that they love them.

I challenge you to restore the beauty of the kiss. It is a harmless, tender, wonderful way to physically connect with someone, without putting someone you love at risk for harm, disease, or life changing consequences.

When people are in love, desire kicks in, and they want to be together, but even a relational morality, one based on love, can have painful consequences. How we understand love can change with our own age and maturity, so even though a relational morality sounds good in theory, it can be very complicated and have negative consequences.

Questions to ponder:

1. Is sex the best way for two people in love, who are not married, to show the depth of their love?

2. Have you ever thought you were in love, but in a few months, you found you had nothing in common with each other?

"When I love, someone and promise to love him/her forever, is sex OK even if we are not married?"

Chapter 19. A Third Choice Is Still Complicated

To review, a Recreational Morality says that sex is always right, never wrong; it is the "If it feels good, do it" mentality. A Relational Morality says that when you love someone, sex is a beautiful expression of that love and therefore, cannot be wrong.

A Committal Morality says that sex is only all that it was created to be, a sacred gift, when two people love each other and profess that love to God, with a forever commitment, ideally within the sacrament of Marriage.

He was a senior, and she was a freshman. He was a great guy who was captivated by her beauty. If he had chosen a recreational morality, he would have asked her out, and they would've had sex. If she had a recreational morality, she probably would have said, "yes," because he was a senior, and she would have thought it was so cool that a senior liked her, a mere freshman. She might have thought she would have lost him if she had refused to have sex.

As it was, she was not pressured to have sex with him, because he truly respected women and the sacredness of sex. Although a senior, a football player, and a great looking guy, he was a virgin. He had chosen a committal morality and had planned to save sex for marriage.

They dated throughout his last year of high school. He helped her deal with the adjustments of being a freshman: choosing classes, dealing with teachers, balancing her schedule, getting along with her parents, and dealing with the drama always created by her friends. They talked about everything and had so much fun together. She was as special as she was beautiful!

He graduated from high school and went off to college. He encouraged her to enjoy all that high school had to offer and was not possessive or controlling of her in anyway. He loved her and realized that she needed to experience high school and college before he could marry her anyway. His was a very healthy, unselfish love, and he knew in his heart that someday she would be his wife.

When he was a senior in college and she was a senior in high school, they realized that they had shared everything for four years: dreams, hopes, fears, joys, and sorrows. Their love had deepened each year, and they had grown to admire and respect each other for who they were. They were truly in love, so they decided that the time was right to make love. That physical intimacy was very special to both of them; they were committed to each other; they loved each other deeply, and they wanted to become one physically with one another.

It was July 7. I came running into the house for a quick shower after a very hot tennis match. The phone rang. I hesitated to answer it because I just wanted a cool shower. By the grace of God, I answered the phone.

Someone was crying on the line. I couldn't identify the voice, but he said that he was just calling to say goodbye. My reaction was one of confusion for a second, and then alarm set in.

"I am going to kill myself. I just can't handle it anymore. I am such a terrible person. I don't deserve to live."

"Wait a minute", I said. "Who is this? Please try to calm yourself down. I want to help you. Please don't hang up, and please don't hurt yourself. I care about you."

He started to talk through his tears. He told me it was the one year anniversary of the day he took his girlfriend to have an abortion. During that year his sister gave birth to a baby, and whenever he saw his niece he couldn't stand the guilt. Every baby he has seen for the entire year was a painful reminder of what he had chosen to do. He had killed his baby, acting against everything he had ever believed about life, when he had given into the demands of the girl he loved.

"I can't be pregnant right now," his girlfriend frantically screamed at him. "You don't understand! I am only a senior in high school. I want

to go to college next year. I don't want this baby! If you love me, you will take me to have an abortion!"

He did love her, more than anything. What was she saying? Neither of them believed in abortion. They had planned to marry someday, and they both wanted children. Though at first shaken by the news of her pregnancy and very surprised, because he had always used protection, and they had only made love three times over the three months since they had decided to deepen their relationship through sex, he was not that upset.

"Please relax, honey, I love you. I am going to graduate from college and a couple of weeks. I will get a good job, and we can get married like we had planned. I will take care of you. We will be a family. I will support you while you take night classes. You can still go to college. It will be okay, I promise."

She screamed hysterically, "I don't want to go to night classes! I want to go to college and have fun. I can't have this baby! I am not ready to get married. I love you, and if you love me you will understand, that I can't be pregnant right now!"

"But you are pregnant, and it will be okay. I am ready to be a husband and a father. We love each other. This is what we have been waiting for. We have dated for four years. I love you, and you love me."

For a few weeks, they were both frantic. He was trying to convince her that everything would be fine, and she insisted that if he loved her, he would take her for an abortion. Afterwards, she promised that they would just go on dating until she graduated from college. Nothing would change their love.

Because he did love her; he couldn't stand to see her so distressed. He took her for an abortion. Immediately, they were no longer comfortable with each other. It was as though they couldn't look at each other. They had compromised their values. They felt like partners in crime. They had created a life, and destroyed it. Everything had changed!

The call from this young professional one year later was gut wrenching for me. I ached for this young man who had impeccable character and was such a mess because he had given into the pressure of an abortion.

Thank God we talked and talked for hours that day, and I persuaded him not to kill himself. For months we dealt with his pain, his heartache, and his guilt. Because we both believed in a merciful God, I was able to convince him that God still loved him, and he was worthy of life, love, and happiness in his future.

He talked with a priest and received the sacrament of Reconciliation. The hardest parts of his healing were forgiving himself, and losing the woman he loved because of their mistake. They tried to date again, but it didn't work out because they were no longer living and loving as they had planned, in accordance with their beliefs.

The baby was created out of love, by a couple with a committed morality. Why wasn't there the joy and ecstasy God desires for us in the deep intimacy of making love?

Apparently, something was missing.

Questions to ponder:

1. When is timing important as a factor in your decision making? Can something seem right and be wrong at the same time?

2. When you have to make a major decision, do you have a plan in place for the process?

Try this acronym to guide you in decision making: STOP

S Search out the facts

T Think about alternatives and consequences

O consider and consult with Others

P Pray for wisdom, courage, and direction

Chapter 20. Suicide Is Never the Solution

That last chapter was very difficult for me to write. It is filled with pain, and not just his pain, but my pain. I had been extremely close to this young man throughout his high school career, and even before. I couldn't understand why he hadn't come to me for help when he and his girlfriend were struggling with their surprise pregnancy.

Eventually, I asked him.

He told me he hadn't come to me because I always encourage teenagers to be chaste, and he didn't want to disappoint me. He thought I would think less of him. He was embarrassed and ashamed. He did not want to let me down.

Now, here is a very important lesson: suicide is a permanent solution to a temporary problem. It is never a good idea.

When people love you, they will try to guide you to make life decisions and to choose a code of morality, which will bring you the least pain in your life and the most love. They do not expect perfection when they present you with the ideals, and they will always be there to support you when you fail. They will love you through whatever pain you feel.

All problems are survivable when you share them. Suicide is never a solution. When you feel overwhelmed or without hope, seek help, please.

By sharing his pain, and finally, feeling some relief because of God's mercy and self-forgiveness, he was able to go on.

Every year while I worked at his Alma Mater, he sent me a check to give to a needy student to cover the cost of a ticket to the annual

Mother/Son Dinner Dance, and then another check to give another needy student for the Father/Daughter Dinner Dance. He didn't know the gender of the child he had created, but to commemorate the life of his son or daughter whom he would never know on this earth, but would forever love, his generous offer celebrated his/her life.

No matter what mistakes you make, you are always loved.

Questions to ponder:

1. Have you ever thought life was too hard to continue living?

2. Ideals are what we strive for, but most often don't attain. Is it hard for you to accept your mistakes or your failures? Remember, we were not created to be perfect. We were created to love, and that means being companions on our shared journeys.

"Aunt Pam, I didn't know you could love someone the second I knew they existed." (Godson's comment when he found out he and his wife were pregnant.)

Chapter 21. The Joy of a Committed Morality

Marriage provides special strengths and graces to allow us to love selflessly and mercifully. Chastity is a virtue, which helps us to love the right person, in the right way, at the right time.

It was June. The school year was ending, and I was eagerly awaiting the birth of my nephew's baby. Mike and his wife Nicole were due anytime. My nephew was a very special man whose smile and goodness melted my heart from the time he was a little boy, and I was his Godmother at his Baptism.

It was a hot, muggy day.

When I rounded the corner, I saw a senior sitting on the bench by the exit outside my office door. I sat down next to him because I noticed that he was as white as a ghost, and he was shaking and sweating. He told me he was going home, and I immediately told him that I could not let him drive in his condition. I encouraged him to come into my office.

When he sat on the couch, his shaking became more violent, and he began to rock back and forth. Scared, I asked if I should call 911. He said that 911 was not going to help him, and he began to cry.

Through his sobs, he blurted out his story. "You know I won a Division I football scholarship?"

I told him that I had heard that good news. I told him how proud I was of him because I knew how hard he had worked. I knew that wasn't the reason for his emotional distress, so I gently asked what it was that had him so upset.

Totally distraught, he spoke in a rambling manner: "I can't go to college now! I love her! My parents are going to kill me! What am I going to tell my Grandma; she thinks I am perfect; she will be so disappointed in me! How can I leave her? I love her so much!" Then, he could speak no more, and he cried uncontrollably.

I knew that he had been dating a classmate for a couple of years. I asked how she was, and his sobbing approached hysteria. He told me that she had just told him that she was late; that she had taken a pregnancy test, and it was positive. He was going to be a father.

These two seniors had proclaimed a love and commitment for life together in marriage. They chose to marry; he gave up his scholarship because he did not believe it would be right for him to go off to play a game while she was left to have their baby on her own. He went to a community college and got a full time job. They thought they were mature enough to handle a family, that their love would get them through, and though not according to plans or according to their schedule, they would make it work. They really tried.

Within two years after their son was born, they began to resent each other. Each regretted that their dreams were not being lived and sadly, they each began to resent their son. They divorced and the grandparents took turns caring for and loving their son.

Although they were ready to promise forever at their young age, they were not able to live forever. Engaging in the sacred act of sex, created to be unitive and co-creative in marriage, is not magical; each person is supposed to bring the best version of himself/herself into a marriage. That development takes time and it means discovering who you are, becoming who you are supposed to be through education and life experiences, and discovering that true commitment, unselfish love, and service to one another is required in marriage.

Although they loved each other and had promised to love each other forever, they were so very young, and so much personal growth needed to occur before they were ready to make a life long commitment. Mike and Nicole's committal morality was different.

My sister called to tell me my nephew and his wife were in labor at a hospital near to me. I headed there to wait in the lobby. When Mike came out to tell me he had a daughter, he was elated, smiling as broadly as I had ever seen. (He was a Marine pilot, so the smiles of his youth had turned into a certain tough façade, out of necessity.)

When I saw his wife, she was exhausted, but beaming with joy. Mike took his daughter, wrapped in her white blanket, with a pink bow stuck to her bald head, and cradled her in his arms like a football. I noticed her looking at him, as he drew his face close to hers in the deepest love.

I said, "Mikey, she is looking at you!" (Babies often don't wake up or focus right away.) I think she recognizes you."

He said, "Of course she knows me, Aunt Pam, I am her daddy, and she is my little girl."

My heart was overwhelmed by the obvious love he felt for her. He went on to describe how he had read to her, sang to her, talked to her, and even told her a joke or two; from the second he knew she existed, he celebrated her and loved her.

He told me, he didn't realize he could love anyone instantly, from the moment they came into existence. He described how he had to grow in his love for his wife, who he treasured, valued, and loved so deeply, but with Brie, his little girl, love was instantaneous.

I believe Mike's awesome, ecstatic feeling is the joy which God desires for us as humans when we discover that we are co-creators of life with him. Parenthood is the most other-centered of loves, the way our heavenly Father loves and treasures each one of us, as if we were his only child, his first-born, the way Mike loved Brie!

This is the love I wish for you, one that feeds your inner core with joy. You have the choice to either experience that instant joy when you discover that you are pregnant or that your wife is pregnant, or to experience the panic, anxiety, distress and fear that happens when you discover that you are late or your girlfriend is late.

Choosing chastity can increase your chances of finding authentic, real love. It is a virtue that you can grow in, like honesty. Just because you have lied, does not mean that you can never be an honest person. Just because you engaged in sex or sexual stimulation for personal pleasure, or out of a mistaken belief in a forever love, doesn't mean you can never live a chaste life again.

Sometimes we discover the power of sex the hard way. The same way we can come to a deeper understanding of the impact sex can have on our lives, we can learn what real love is.

You can grow in chastity. You can discover the peace and joy, which you were designed to feel, when you eliminate the risks of a recreational or even a relational morality. By choosing chastity and waiting for marriage, you will be less likely to experience the pain of a betrayal after a premature commitment, the panic accompanying an unplanned pregnancy, the physical pain of a sexually transmitted disease, or the emotional trauma of a broken heart because your body promised forever, before you were ready.

As long as you can breathe and think, you can choose to change. We have a God of do-overs, of unconditional love and infinite mercy.

Choose a committal morality. Choose chastity.

Questions to ponder:

1. Do you think chastity is worth striving for?

2. Do you really believe you can choose to change, to be different? I do.

"The day the power of love overrules the love of power, the world will know peace."

Gandhi

Chapter 22. Things That Work against Love

Sometimes society accidentally contributes to negativity when sharing messages about relationships, family, and love. Twenty-four hour news coverage and instantaneous information, which is available on all of our social media devices, have affected us.

Stories of celebrity wealth, pictures of beautiful models, scenes about passion, and tweets from superstar singers, dancers, athletes, and other performers can make other peoples' lives seem glamorous and desirable. Our lives in comparison may feel empty, insignificant, unsuccessful, lonely, and isolated.

At times, it is difficult to read others' posts or check out pictures on Facebook and not feel a twinge of envy. Questions like "Is this all there is?" about one's own life may be contributing to sadness, depression, and a sense of failure.

When you get stuck in the comparison game, you may feel inferior to your friends or even their friends' friends, people whom you don't even know. If you measure your worth or identity by comparing yourself to others, you will always feel miserable. You can always find someone whose life seems better than yours, but people wear masks, and what they post or show the world is probably not their truth in the real sense of the word.

What do I mean? It is kind of like the Christmas letters people often write which share all the wonderful accomplishments of each family member. They don't share their struggles in their marriage, arguments with their assertive teen, battles with alcohol, food, or drug addiction, mental illness, or academic challenges.

They don't share nights of screaming and domestic violence, or twenty-four hours in the local jail for a fight with a local gang, or a juvenile arrest for shoplifting. They don't share that they caught their child smoking weed, or in bed with a boyfriend. Life is not easy or perfect for any of us.

Sometimes, people with whom we come in contact can feed us with self doubt, negative coping mechanisms, and a sense of hopelessness. These people are hurting and could use your help, but only if you are strong enough to rise above their dark view of life and the world to show them a different way.

You must become the best version of yourself to inspire them to choose to change. You cannot change another person, but sometimes people who are lost can contribute to you losing your way. Be careful of what or whom you allow to shape your life.

By finding people worthy of trust in your life, people who will honor your confidentiality, and genuinely advise and support you as you grow, you can become a major catalyst for change. You will be contributing to a more loving, supportive, and kind world.

Some of you may be blessed with families, who have modeled kindness, commitment, acceptance, appreciation, individuality, respect, empowerment, mercy, and honest communication. You may have experienced, first hand, what genuine love looks like in family relationships.

Many have not seen true love modeled and are craving that authenticity. That searching, that desire are why I believe the TV show, This Is Us, is so popular? This series is affecting viewers by taking us to raw, honest emotions about family love, invoking in both men and women a deep connection with the characters and their stories.

Why are these characters and their open honest stories getting into our very souls? I think it is because each character's flaws and goodness are displayed. Each messes up and each beautifully comforts another in an unpredictable, but very believable way. Each person tries to do what is right and good and sometimes succeeds and sometimes fails. Family members and friends disappoint one another sometimes, and other times mercifully love and forgive one another.

Priorities change because of insights gained from life experiences, and from observing, and listening to one another. Characters sometimes feel unappreciated, guilty, betrayed, abandoned, and wounded by one another, but through open, honest communication, healing occurs and love flows.

Love requires honesty and vulnerability. Being vulnerable means "able to be hurt." Anytime, we open ourselves to love, we are certainly risking pain, betrayal, misunderstanding, or rejection. However, if we don't open our hearts to love, we will never know the intimacy, the unconditional forgiveness, the total acceptance, and the joy, which comes from being truly loved by another.

Questions to ponder:

1. Your parents, who are imperfect people like you, can teach you who you want to be, and who you don't want to be? Would you like some things to be different in your own family someday?

2. Who or what in your life, builds you up? Who or what beats you down? Choices, decisions, and consequences are real. Think about what changes you can make to enable your journey toward love and happiness to be more easily attainable.

Section III. The Plan

Practical Ideas to Help You Find Real Love

"Watch your thoughts, for they become words. Watch your words, for they become actions. Watch your actions, for they become habits. Watch your habits, for they become character. Watch your character, for it becomes your destiny."

Unknown

Chapter 23. You Can Do It!

All major religious traditions teach basically the same message: love, compassion, and forgiveness must be a part of our everyday lives, if we are to find the joy and peace that God desires for us to share with Him. That joy comes from healthy love relationships groomed by an understanding of what real love is.

Let us take a look at some steps you can take to increase your chances of finding ideal love. Of course, everyone has a choice everyday to help their relationships grow or to let them wilt and die. We have to accept that we cannot control the choices, which others make, so sometimes even the most loving people end up being hurt by a broken relationship. The one thing we can control is our choices. The following suggestions can increase your chances of discovering real love.

I. Believe that you are worthy of love and capable of loving.

Ten Steps To Help You Feel Good about Yourself

1. Love yourself. Make a list of all of your good qualities, talents, and gifts. If this is difficult for you to do, ask people you love and respect to help you discover those things about you, and believe them when they are saying good things about you. (Sometimes it is hard to believe good things about yourself especially if you have been broken by abuse, rejection, or repeated failures or mistakes, for which you have not forgiven yourself.)

2. Identify the qualities, the virtues, and the values most important to you. If money, popularity, drugs, alcohol, sex

and other stuff is not "doing it" for you, try reflecting on this message from St. Augustine: "There is a God-shaped hole in the heart of everyone that cannot be filled by anything but God, if we want to experience the joy, love, and peace that God desires for us in this world." If how we live is not bringing us joy, peace, and love, we might want to re-evaluate and make some changes.

3. Find people who share those values and virtues with you, so you don't feel weird or strange. Feeling odd or different can sometimes cause people to feel unworthy of love. Sometimes, feeling that way causes people to do things against their beliefs to try to fit in.

4. Do community service. Volunteer. Share your gifts and talents with the world. It is amazing how good it feels to help others. Helping others is a beautiful way to feel significant and to discover what a positive impact you can have on the world. Find your passion; support a cause in which you believe. Make a difference.

5. Look in the mirror everyday and do positive self- talk. You are beautiful. You are gifted. You are talented. You are capable. You are loveable. Keep telling yourself these things until you believe that you are beautifully and wonderfully made.

6. Surround yourself with people who are striving to be the best version of themselves in the same way you are trying to grow into the best version of yourself.

7. Choose to never be bored. Boredom is an attitude, which prevents you from seeing the many opportunities available to you to grow physically, intellectually, emotionally, relationally, and spiritually each day.

8. Watch what you watch. Social media and 24 hour news coverage can sometimes give you a twisted, negative view of life. When we focus on darkness, it is difficult to see the light.

9. Look at each other eyeball to eyeball, heart to heart. When we notice each other, we connect in a way that brings people to friendship and kind, loving relationships.

10. Try not to be judgmental. Look for the good in others. Give people who have hurt you or disappointed you "do-overs." Nobody is perfect, and since hatred hurts the hater, choose to forgive others. You will feel lighter emotionally, and will more easily see the good in others, despite their struggles and their mistakes.

II. Make sure your relationships are healthy.

All relationships range from healthy to abusive. There are degrees of unhealthy somewhere in the middle. When you feel good about yourself, it is easier to expect certain qualities in your relationships. You will realize that you are deserving of respect, that your opinion matters in conversations, that you are entitled to have both same gender and opposite gender relationships without someone being jealous or controlling of your time.

You will realize that trust, honesty, and open communication are essential ingredients in healthy relationships. You will believe that touch should be respectful, gentle, non-demanding, and mutually agreed upon. In healthy relationships, people are not controlling, violent, or possessive.

Steps to Assure That Your Relationships Are Healthy

1. Don't ever sell yourself short. Do everything you can to become a confident, assertive individual who knows what you believe in, what you stand for, and how you want to live your life, as you grow into adulthood. If you have trouble believing that you are a good person worthy of friends, and deserving of love and respect, seek counseling or take leadership classes and assertiveness classes. Believe that you

are good, and that you are both capable of and deserving of love.

2. Surround yourself with good people. Ask yourself if you are a better person when you hang with someone, and if you are not, perhaps you should distance yourself until you can maintain your confidence and your authenticity, even in that person's presence.

3. Strive for and treasure honesty in your relationships. If your friend asks you to lie for him/her about where they are or what they are doing, ask yourself if you value honesty in friendships, and if you do, seek other relationships.

4. Be kind and have fun. Is the time you spend together fun, uplifting, and respectful of others, or are you making fun of others or bullying others as your form of entertainment?

5. Have friends who support your decisions and have a good influence on you. Are you being pressured to make decisions about drugs, alcohol, or sex which you would not want the person, whom you admire and respect the most, to know you are doing?

6. Share in-depth conversations about sex, love, dating, and other life issues with your parents, who can help you on your journey to developing healthy relationships. Healthy touch and hugs are important; hug your family.

7. Let your parents know your friends: have them over to your house and play a game or have dinner together, so you can observe if they are the same with your parents as they are with you. You will benefit from having authentic friends.

8. Get involved in your church, synagogue, temple, mosque, or place of worship, so you can develop spiritually and address issues not only of this world, but also of the next. Often you will find a friend in these faith experiences who will help you to grow spiritually.

9. Be physically active, get involved in volunteer opportunities, help each other with homework, and support each other's growth and successes.

10. Always pray to have eyes that see the best in people, a heart that forgives the worst, a mind that forgets the bad, and a soul that never loses faith in God.

III. Date the Right Way

When I first starting giving talks to teenagers about love, sex, and developing a personal morality, which would directly affect your physical, emotional, and spiritual health, the response from adolescence was quite different than it is now. Teens used to think meaningless, non-relational sex was taboo, but now often times they see no relationship between love and sex.

Dating the right way can be a fun, pressure free, activity to learn about yourself, your date, and the opposite sex. By setting boundaries for intimacy, there will be near zero risk for any long-term pain, damage, or risks.

Suggestions for Healthy Dating

1. Don't rush dating. You will change a great deal in the next few years, and the changes will be most obvious once you turn 16. Your brain makes some major changes, starting at this age, regarding your ability to abstractly think, (What is love? What is integrity? What does commitment mean?) to assess danger, and to understand cause and effect, and will continue to change until the ages of 26-33.

2. Understand the risks of oral sex, masturbation, sexting, and pornography and avoid them. Be honest, research the negative impact, and believe me when I say, you will be healthier and happier if you avoid these activities.

3. Don't spend hours alone with someone you are physically attracted to. Sex is a powerful drive, and it is difficult to control, even if you have decided to wait for sex. It is like playing with fire: how close can you get before you get burned?

4. Avoid dating if you are under the influence of alcohol or other drugs. The number of people with whom I have met during my years in ministry who have stated, "I didn't mean for it to happen," regarding sexual activities, is huge. Alcohol combined with hormones, curiosity, physical attraction, desire, or even love is not a good combination, if you want to be in charge of your decisions.

5. Recognize teen-dating violence for what it is: date rape is rampant because people get themselves in compromising situations, and don't realize that No means No. Sometimes people receive mixed messages, and choose not to stop. Remember sex is a powerful drive! Never let anyone hit you, slap you, push you, physically or emotionally hurt you with their words or actions. Don't believe it when then tell you they love you, and they are sorry and promise never do it again. Don't date them again. Run, and seek help professionally and legally. Tell your parents or an adult whom you trust and who wants what is best for you.

6. Group date. Always have a trusted friend with you to protect you if you are about to do something you have said you didn't believe in or would never do.

7. Set boundaries with your date in advance of any physical contact. If you cannot agree, date someone else because this date doesn't honor and respect your wishes.

8. When dating, always work on finding balance: one night of a weekend, have a date, one night a weekend hang out with same gender friends, and one night a week hang out together with family, playing games, sharing dinner, just getting to know each others history through stories, which might be

told by parents or siblings. The time with family will also show you how and if they respect their parents and siblings; these behaviors are important indicators of how they will treat you.

9. Take it slow when dating. Don't trust someone right away with your secrets, dreams, fears, struggles, successes, or failures. Knowing someone takes time, so don't promise forever or dream of forever with someone you don't really know. Commitment before sex is the ideal for happiness.

10. Knowledge of someone's values, character, and beliefs, is necessary before trust is deserved, and trust is necessary before reliance is a good idea. Trustworthiness and reliability should be proven before any commitment is made.

IV. Believe in Marriage.

Marital love for many is the ultimate goal. Why is it so difficult for people to stay married in the USA in today's world when people need nothing more than to feel loved, safe, and secure?

Maybe, it is because sex is no longer the sacred gift people eagerly anticipated experiencing with one another for the first time on their wedding night. (Sex has become so routine that whole wedding parties are often invited on a couple's honeymoon.)

Maybe, it is because the passion of sex is so accessible in so many forms of media that married couples think they are missing out on something. Because sometimes when they make love, it is not the crazy, passionate, multi- orgasmic act depicted in movies and other media, they may seek other people to sleep with outside of their marriage.

Maybe, it is because we have moved away from God who is the source of all love, and are no longer a part of a Church family to support us in our marriage covenant.

Maybe, it is because people view aging as something to avoid:

so many seek Botox, and other cosmetic surgeries in an attempt to stay forever young, and so they desire to have a youthful partner.

Maybe, it is because we have forgotten how to think of others first; so many have to be the center of attention…making everything, which used to be private, public on Facebook or in other ways drawing attention to themselves.

Maybe, it is because people have lost hope, and they don't believe everlasting love is even possible. If you don't believe it is possible, you won't attain it!

These are some pointers for finding Mr. or Miss Right.

How to Find the Best Girl/Guy to Marry

1. Become the best guy or girl. Become the person God created you to be in all four categories of personhood: physical, intellectual, social (relational and emotional) and spiritual.

2. Strive for chastity. Chastity is a virtue, which allows you to love God, yourself, and another, and love the beautiful sacredness of sex in a selfless, loving way. A virtue is an ideal in which you can grow, like honesty. (Just because you have told a lie, doesn't mean you will be forever dishonest.) If you have attained every other level of intimacy other than the physical, you will have reached a oneness where when sex or physical intimacy is added, it is the icing on the cake, not the cake. Your foundation will be much more solid.

3. Share dreams, hopes, fears, failures, struggles, and successes with one another, before you share anything physical.

4. Work through reconciliation after a disagreement, before you share anything physical. Find out how the other fights, and if it is belittling, berating, verbally or physically violent, get out.

5. Visit with the other's family often. Listen to childhood stories told by parents or siblings and observe how your date treats other family members.

6. Observe how he/she treats waiters and waitresses in a restaurant, ushers in a play, people of other races, religions, or ethnicities, the rich and famous, or people who are poor or homeless.
7. Talk about religion, beliefs and values, family ideals, and visions of marriage.
8. Do service together, work together on a project, discuss a book, talk about movies after you view them together: really get to know each other.
9. Pray together, and for each other to be the best version of who each of you was created to be.
10. Pray that your parents stay married. Give the suggestions below to them, because one of the best things for you would be to live in a home where parents love and respect one another and honor their wedding vows.

Suggestions for Finding Wedded Bliss in Marriage

1. See each other as good, but recognize that neither of you will ever be perfect.
2. Treat each other with kindness and respect.
3. Listen to each other with your ears, your mind, and your heart.
4. Be present to each other daily. If work schedules or geographical distance keeps you apart, text, tweet, write, call, or at the very least pray for each other daily.
5. Smile at each other whenever you see each other and make eye contact. Go on regular dates with each other.
6. Don't keep score or try to be equal in all that you contribute to your relationship. Someone said. "Divorce is 50-50, but marriage is 100-100% in giving and sharing.
7. Be willing to apologize and be willing to forgive.

8. Be open with each other and trust your love, by laughing together, working toward goals together, even crying together, if life gets rough or you feel broken.

9. Seek help if you feel lonely, disappointed, or distant from one another, so those negative emotions don't consume you.

10. Hug and kiss for at least 30 seconds every day, even if you feel tired, overwhelmed, or a little mad, especially before you go to bed.

Questions to Ponder:

1. What is one suggestion from each group, which you could focus on first? Take one step at a time toward the attainment of your goals.

2. Can you already look back on the experiences of your life and realize each experience has taught you something? What experience has been the most helpful for you as you have traveled to this point on your journey?

Pam Heil

Each day compare yourself to the person you were the day before. Are you kinder, more confident, more productive, more unselfish, more helpful, more loving, more forgiving? Try to be better tomorrow.

Chapter 24. Be the Best Version of Yourself You Can Be

Sometimes we can get trapped in the comparison game. We measure our worth in comparisons with others. We might check out other people's posts, tweets, snap chats or whatever and give them too much influence on how we feel about ourselves. Comparing ourselves to others is a fleeting past time, which can take us to a sense of pride or a sense of helplessness. Comparisons can make us feel hopeless and defeated, or can even make us feel complacent and cocky.

Comparing yourself with yourself by checking out how you are living each day, how you are seizing opportunities, how you are handling defeats, how you are treating others, how you are taking care of yourself, and how you are growing in wisdom, kindness, and grace, can help you become a better version of yourself each day.

Several years ago, I was struck by a young woman who understood the impact of words on her feelings and actions. When she went to college, which she believed would be a challenging time, she chose to decorate her dorm room with positive, inspirational quotes. Many other young co-eds decorated their rooms with alcohol commercials, sexually provocative posters of physically attractive people, and sometimes even messages of profanity.

I am sure in the beginning some of her acquaintances might have thought she was a goody, goody, maybe even a little weird.

After a few months of the freedom and temptations of college life, and perhaps having made some decisions, which might have taken them to a dark, disappointing place, some of the girls would actually come to this young lady's dorm room and ask if they could lay on her bed and read her walls. They needed lifted up. Some needed forgiveness and the confidence to begin again. The messages on the walls gave them hope and healing.

Surrounding ourselves with any form of media, which lifts us up, gives us hope, inspires us to greatness, or helps us become better citizens of the world is a great tool for personal growth. Anything, which helps us to discover the good within ourselves, and how to most effectively share it with others, is a good thing, in my opinion.

I have been inspired by everyday people and people of renown. Reby, a summer camp counselor, made me feel special when she wrote me a letter from college when I was just 5 years old. Joyce helped me believe that I could go to college, the first one in my family to do so. Fritz and Larry coordinated my job schedules, which allowed me to work two 40 hour jobs in the summer to pay my way through college. Mama T. became a surrogate mom for me showing me how to be gracious, classy, and kind. Sister Josetta encouraged me to be a speaker on issues of sex, love, and marriage. Wonderful teachers helped to expand my mind and my dreams. Spiritual directors like Fathers Fred, Bob, and Steve, Rachel, my first director of Religious Education who introduced me to the Bible, and Clau my first Bible Study facilitator and SBK (Spiritual Butt Kicker) helped me feed my spiritual entity.

I have been inspired by Mother Teresa of Calcutta who proclaims the relevance of everything we do each day; she acknowledged that even though we may not all do great things, we can do all things, even the most mundane, with unselfish love. Her writings challenge me to be nice, to be honest, to be forgiving, and to be helpful even when others aren't. She encourages me to be happy by being grateful for the many blessings I have been given, and to choose to be positive and joyful.

From Martin Luther King I learned that change can be made peacefully. Inspired by him, I have become a good listener and respect differences in people, while still celebrating our shared humanity. I realize that hatred hurts the hater and only through love can we bring light into darkness.

From authors like Maya Angelou I have been reminded how each of us can bring sunshine to someone who has been beaten down by life, by being present to them. I realize that by calling people by name, looking them in the eye, warmly shaking their hands or hugging them, people will feel connected, and people will always remember how you make them feel.

Our world needs you to be a source of positive energy. We need you to spread kindness, love, and mercy to everyone with whom you come in contact. We need you to search for the good in others, instead of focusing on any bad, which they may have shown you. We need you to be respectful of others and to challenge others without judging them.

We need you to forgive yourself from mistakes you have made and to learn from them. We need you to always believe you are worthy of love and respect. We need you to be responsible and productive, to work hard, and to be accountable. We need you to be a person of integrity: one who knows what you believe and one who lives by those beliefs, whether or not anybody is watching.

I am going to share with you a few more of my favorite inspirational and thought-provoking messages. I know you can Google any that speak to you and your values, but these have shaped me, and they seem to have passed the test of time.

I hope they help you the way they have helped me become a person I love and respect today... ME!

I am a child of God, beautifully and wonderfully made! Though still imperfect, I am OK!

The Serenity Prayer

God, grant me the serenity to accept the things I cannot change, the courage to change the things I can, and the wisdom to know the difference. (Reinhold Niebuhr)

The Difference

I got up early one morning and rushed right into the day. I had so much to accomplish that I didn't have time to pray.

Problems just tumbled about me and heavier came each task "Why doesn't God help me?" I wondered.

He answered, "You didn't ask!"

I wanted to see joy and beauty, but the day toiled on, grey and bleak.

I wondered why God didn't show me. He said, "But you didn't seek."

I tried to come into God's presence. I used all my keys at the lock. God lovingly and gently chided, "My child, you didn't knock."

I woke up early this morning and paused before entering the day.

I had so much to accomplish that I had to take time to pray. (Anonymous)

The Thomas Merton Prayer

My Lord God, I have no idea where I am going. I do not see the road ahead of me. I cannot know for certain where it will end.

Nor do I really know myself, and the fact that I think I am following your will does not mean that I am actually doing so.

But I believe that the desire to please you does in fact please you. And I hope I have that desire in all that I am doing.

I hope that I will never do anything apart from that desire. And I know that if I do this, you will lead me by the right road, though I may know nothing about it.

Therefore, I will trust you always though I may seem to be lost and in the shadow of death.

I will not fear for you are ever with me, and you will never leave me to face my perils alone.

Prayer of St. Francis

Lord, make me an instrument of your peace.

Where there is hatred, let me sow love.

Where there is injury... pardon.

Where there is discord... unity.

Where there is doubt... faith.

Where there is error… truth.

Where there is despair… hope.

Where there is sadness… joy.

Where there is darkness… light.

O Divine Master, Grant that I may never so much seek to be consoled as to console.

To be understood… as to understand.

To be loved… as to love.

For it is in giving… that we receive.

It is in pardoning… that we are pardoned.

It is in dying… that we are born to eternal life.

Mahatma Gandhi

"You must be the change you wish to see in the world."

Nelson Mandela

"Courage is not the absence of fear, but the triumph over it."

John F. Kennedy

"Ask not what your country can do for you, but what you can do for your country."

Buddha

"Happiness never decreases by being shared."

"Better that a thousand hollow words is one word that brings peace."

Dalai Lama

"If you want others to be happy, practice compassion. If you want to be happy, practice compassion."

"Love and compassion are necessities, not luxuries. Without them, humanity cannot survive."

"When you practice gratefulness, there is a sense of respect toward others."

Theodore Roosevelt

"Believe you can, and you are halfway there."

Ralph Waldo Emerson

"What lies behind you and what lies in front of you, pales in comparison to what lies inside of you."

St. Jerome

"Good, better, best; never let it rest. Till your good is better and your better, best."

Favorite Quotes and Teachings by Jesus Christ

"A new command I give you: Love one another. As I have loved you, so must you love one another." John 13:34

"Love your enemies, and pray for those who persecute you." Matthew 5:44

"Blessed are the merciful, for they will be shown mercy." Matthew 5:7

"Let the one among you who is without sin be the first to cast a stone." John 8:7

"You must love your neighbor as you love yourself." Lev.19:18; Matt. 5:43; Mark12:31; Luke 10:27; Romans 13:9; Galatians 5:14; James 2:8

"For everyone who exalts himself will be humbled, and everyone who humbles himself will be exalted." Luke 14:11

"I am the Way, the Truth, and the Life." John 14:16

"Eye has not seen, ear has not heard what God has in store for those who love him." 1 Corinthians 2:9

"Do to others as you would have them do to you." Luke 6:31

From the teachings of Jesus Christ I hope you are reminded that you are not to be afraid, that he offers you peace each day, and he promises that you will never be alone. I hope you believe that there is nothing you can do to make him love you more, and nothing you can do to make him love you less. He loves you perfectly, and when you believe in that unconditional love in your core of core, you will be better able to accept his challenge for you to love others the same way. I hope that you can be God with skin on in this world. What more do we need than to be bathed by the warmth of God's love!

As you strive to be the best version of yourself, I invite you to search for positive role models. Find your positive media messages and surround yourself with them. Keep them on your phone, your computer, your tablet, and your wall. They really will help you, as mine have helped me.

Questions to ponder:

1. What is a mantra or motto you that you strive to live by?

2. Would your friends think these weird or would they agree with them?

"Two things make me mad. When you lie to me, and when I see someone hurting another person on purpose. There is already enough accidental pain in our relationships; we should never hurt someone on purpose."

Pam Heil

Chapter 25. Find an Accountability Partner

Life is not easy. We live in a world where people can view truth completely differently. The world's values seem to be changing as quickly as your favorite Avatar, Emoji, or I-Phone.

My high school youth and my friends and family can tell you what I believe in, what I stand for, and what makes me angry. I am pretty consistent because I have prayerfully determined what brings me closer to God, and what helps me be a better reflection of God's love and mercy in my world.

It is difficult to determine our purpose and to accomplish our goals. To love as we have been challenged to love; to live the way we desire to live, once we have determined our core values and learned from our mistakes; to become a better version of ourselves each day…these are not easy tasks.

With all things in life, both good and bad, we benefit when we share them with another human being. Having an accountability partner will truly help you grow into the person you are challenging yourself to become.

To find the right people to hold you accountable you must be totally honest with them; you must be transparent and wear no mask; you must be vulnerable. They must know your flaws, your challenges, your weaknesses, and your struggles.

They must know your sins: the things you do to hurt your relationship with God; the things you do to hurt your relationships with others: your parents, your friends, teachers, coaches, significant other, siblings, teammates, colleagues, etc., and they must know any of the things that you are doing to hurt yourself.

It takes courage to be that honest with anyone because there is always the risk of being hurt or betrayed by someone who knows you that well. Take the time to know someone is worthy of that depth of intimacy and friendship before you ask them to be your accountability partner, but try to find someone who will help you on your journey from this point in your life to eternity.

Share your core values with this person of trust. Tell them your physical, intellectual, emotional, relational, and spiritual goals. Ask them to call you out if they observe behaviors, which are moving you away from the attainment of your goals.

Pray with them for guidance and right words, spoken in honesty and out of love. You must trust their love to give them this power. You must believe that any time they challenge you that they are only acting out of love: the Thomas Aquinas love: "To will the good of another." You must believe they only want what is best for you.

They must believe in you and commit to helping you be whoever you strive to be.

I have been blessed with accountability partners at different phases in my life. No matter how much time lapses between conversations or face -to -face encounters with these trusted friends, I feel their genuine love and concern for me. I have found my most trusted friends on retreats, in Bible Study, and on mission trips because we seemed to be sharing the same core values at the root of our friendships. Asking them to hold me accountable seemed safe.

I am a Catholic Christian, and I believe that God loves me deeply, intimately, and unconditionally. I believe he is forever by my side. I even believe he lives within me.

I also believe that we are called to be the hands and feet of Christ in this world of challenges, and I believe that my accountability partners are God with skin on!

Nothing like a good hug!

As you grow and learn how to love deeply and authentically, I wish you patience and mercy with yourself and others, the ability to laugh at your mistakes, but to also learn from them, and the gift of authentic friendships. Remember, to have a friend, you must be a friend.

As I say farewell, I challenge you to believe in the ideal, that real love is possible. Acknowledge the challenges in our culture and in our world and arm yourself with the support and the tools you need to make real love possible in your life.

I will be praying for you, and I invite you to pray for me and for one another.

I have no doubt that genuinely loving one another is possible. You can do it, because we humans, we were created to love, and to be loved! It is how we are wired.

Never forget that God loves you, and it is because he does, that you are capable of loving!

Questions to ponder:

1. What does it mean to truly believe that you are loved?

2. Do you now believe that real love is "for real?"

Conclusion

I believe our world can be transformed by love. People being kind to one another is vital to peace.

Love your neighbor. Celebrating and recognizing diversity will allow you to form relationships with uniquely made people from all different cultures, races, ethnicities, and religions. We all need the same things: to love and to be loved.

Love God. Practice your faith. Live what you believe.

Set goals. Work hard. Be accountable and responsible. Doing these things will help you believe in your value, recognize your worth, and truly love yourself.

Lean on each other. Ask for help when you need it. Don't try to do life on your own.

Be true to yourself. I invite you as young people to do all that you can to be the person you were created to be. Identify your strengths and share your goodness with the world.

In doing so, you can help create the beautiful masterpiece that is possible when we all blend together as one family. Let us celebrate our shared humanity!

I believe in love, and I believe in you!

Peace and Love,
Pam

Printed in the United States
By Bookmasters